"By pulling from her own experiences and gleaning advice from experts, Laura Lee Groves has put together an insightful and fun book on raising boys. She tackles tough topics with wit and wisdom. As a dad, I especially enjoyed the section for fathers at the end of the book and the chapter where Laura's sons talked honestly about growing up."
—Jesse Florea, author and speaker

"This book will reward a mother again and again as she invests time and love in the lives of her boys. Laura Lee Groves writes with warmth and clarity that makes the book a joy to read. And don't be afraid to pass it on to Dad, who will appreciate the unique perspectives that will help every family with boys."
—Sigmund Brouwer, best-selling author of more than forty novels

"Laura Lee Groves's understanding of boys is refreshing, rare, and right on target! Laura teaches you how to bring out the best in your boys . . . and in yourself as a parent. Packed with insight and practical help, *I'm Outnumbered!* shows you how to build the boys you love into responsible, God-honoring men. Moms, for your sake . . . for your sons' sakes . . . read this book."
—Tim Shoemaker, author, speaker, and dad of three grown sons

LAURA LEE GROVES

I'm Outnumbered!

One Mom's Lessons in the Lively Art of Raising Boys

Kregel
Publications

I'm Outnumbered! One Mom's Lessons in the Lively Art of Raising Boys

© 2010 by Laura Lee Groves

Published by Kregel Publications, a division of Kregel, Inc., P.O. Box 2607, Grand Rapids, MI 49501.

Library of Congress Cataloging-in-Publication Data
Groves, Laura Lee, 1956-
I'm outnumbered! : one mom's lessons in the lively art of raising boys / Laura Lee Groves.
    p.   cm.
Includes bibliographical references.
1. Mothers and sons—Religious aspects—Christianity.
2. Child rearing—Religious aspects—Christianity. 3. Groves, Laura Lee, 1956- I. Title.
BV4529.18G76   2010   248.8'431—dc22   2010004763

ISBN 978-0-8254-2739-8

Printed in the United States of America
10 11 12 13 14 / 5 4 3 2 1

Contents

Acknowledgments

People ask how long it took to write this book, and I think, "Well, add up all those years of mothering and ..." But it goes back even further than that. My parents, Merv and Dollye Hendricks, must be thanked for teaching me through their godly parenting. Their love, prayers, and devotion are a part of all I do.

God led me to a wonderful partner in this parenting adventure. John is my biggest blessing in this life—my support, my encourager, my sounding board. What a great role model for our four sons. I cherish him and am thankful every day for his love.

You'll meet our four sons—Jonathan, Matthew, Andrew, and Benjamin—in this book. Life with them has been a roller coaster ride of laughter, tears, and prayer. These four boys left me with wonderful memories and plenty to write about. I'm thankful for their love for family, for their Creator, for each other—and for their hearts to reach out.

Professionally, there are many to thank. The team at Kregel has been great to work with. I'm so thankful for Les Stobbe, my agent, and his heart to help new writers. Without the Florida Christian Writers Conference, this book would never have come to be. Jesse Florea was the first to encourage me to pursue this project, and I appreciate the support he gave that compelled me to go on. The Kindred Heart Writers—Johnnie Donley, Karen Evans, Clella Camp, and Jean Wise—have read every word of this book in various stages and their input and encouragement have been invaluable. I truly could not have done it without the four lovely women who write with me and pray with me.

My biggest thanks and much praise go to my heavenly Father, who enabled me and gave me the grace for this journey. We all need His touch. We're truly outnumbered without it.

Introduction

There you sit—the new mom, rocking your little blue bundle while his big brother plays on the floor nearby. It's an idyllic picture. Suddenly, it hits you—you're now outnumbered. One boy plus one more equals two. Multiple boys, one mom. It doesn't seem like such a big thing now; after all, they're just babies, toddlers. But as those little guys grow, they become more male, and interact in a way that is often foreign to a mom. Trust me... I know. Four boys, all three years apart, interact in my home.

Did I expect to have four children? Yes. Did I expect they'd all be boys? Well ... no. At one point, Jonathan was nine, Matthew was six, Andrew was three, and Benjamin was a newborn. Talk about feeling overwhelmed! Don't get me wrong—multiple boys are wonderful, but that sentiment has come only after lessons learned in twenty-four years of mothering.

Along the way, I've gathered some valuable knowledge from a variety of sources. A father can tell you a lot about raising boys from his perspective, and researchers and psychologists have much to add. Dr. James Dobson's book *Bringing Up Boys* brought our sons' unique challenges to the forefront and provided sound advice. But while a number of men have written on the subject of raising boys, a female voice is lacking.

There are certain things only another "boy mom" knows. I've had my share of mentors—other boy moms whose boys are older—who forged the way. I made numerous phone calls to one or another of them along the way—and honestly, I still do. We laugh, we wonder, we commiserate. In the following pages, I invite you to laugh, to learn, and to wonder with me as I merge boy mom experience with the words of well-known authorities and the ultimate authority, the Word of God.

As you read this book, you can expect to learn and grow and nod your head at times. You'll find stories, quotes, true confessions, and the results of research in these pages. Chapters are short and to the point because I know that a mother's time is precious. When children are around, you grab bits and pieces of a book, rarely a whole chapter at one sitting. You may need to pick and choose chapters in this book, selecting those that speak to where you are at in a particular moment. At best, you'll learn and be encouraged. At least, you'll realize you're not alone in this boy mom adventure, and you'll find yourself able to smile along the way.

You can also expect to learn more about what makes being a boy mom so unique. Stephen James and David Thomas write in their excellent resource *Wild Things: The Art of Nurturing Boys*, "Mothering a boy will require things of you that mothering a daughter will never require."[1] The differences in boys and girls are well-documented. Their minds, their rates of development, their learning styles, their hearts are crafted by God in different ways. Because of those differences, many mothers fail to ever really connect with their sons. This book will give you the tools to better understand your sons and will help you find the best ways to nurture them.

You can expect to be empowered. William Pollack wrote in *Real Boys*, "I believe that by empowering the mother you empower the son. . . . Far from making boys dependent, the base of safety a loving mother can create—a connection that her son can rely on all his life—provides a boy with the courage to explore the outside world."[2] So be empowered, Mom, and empower your sons in return.

Although my words are colored by having mothered four sons, I've found research that speaks to all types of boy moms, and I'll be sharing that with you.

- If you're a mom of "boys plus" (that is, you have a daughter or two in the mix), your experience will be different. You'll find a section here and there that addresses your situation.
- If you're a single mom (that is, widowed, divorced, or never married), read on. Even though there's a husband in my house, much of our experience as mothers of boys will be the same. Appendix C is especially for you, and you'll find some side notes along the way that are relevant to your unique situation.
- Moms with larger families will find that many of the helpful hints in this book can be adapted to a big brood, regardless of your children's gender.

So take heart, Mom—and read on!

1

Great Expectations

You are my lamp, O LORD; the LORD turns my
　　darkness into light.
With your help I can advance against a troop; with
　　my God I can scale a wall.
As for God, his way is perfect; the word of the
　　LORD is flawless.
He is a shield for all who take refuge in him.
　　　　　　　2 SAMUEL 22:29–31

All moms enter parenting with some preconceived notions. Most of us hope to have a mix of blue and pink in the household. We may have expectations for our child's behavior or personality. We may be especially baffled by a little boy whose actions and reactions are so different from ours as a child. A valuable lesson for the mother of multiple boys is that expectations can be a trap. Expectations say, "I have this figured out. I know what will suit me, what I want, what is best for my life." Check those verses at the start of this chapter again: "You are my lamp, O LORD; the LORD turns my darkness into light. With your help I can advance against a troop; with my God I can scale a wall. As for God, his way is perfect; the word of the LORD is flawless. He is a shield for all who take refuge in him."

Scripture can help us through the trap of expectations, the snare of "I know best." King David has some reminders for us:

- God is our lamp. He lights our way, no matter how large a flashlight we try to carry.
- God helps us advance against a troop and scale a wall. We can do it, but we don't do it on our own.
- God's way—not ours—is perfect. He gives us what we need, not what we expect or desire.
- If we hide in Him, He will be our shield. He will protect us.

He provides light, help, a shield, and refuge. And His way—not ours—is perfect.

Maybe You Were Expecting...

... a Girl!

Maybe you were expecting a girl the first time... or the second time... or...!

I know how it is. I had the "girl name" all picked out, too— four times. I haven't given up hope, though. I'm hanging on to it for the first granddaughter.

The first shattered expectation a boy mom often faces is that she's outnumbered in this whole thing called family. With two boys and a husband in the picture, the opportunity for female companionship grows pale. Those little blue bundles tend to destroy our maternal expectations fraught with pink ribbons, lace, and tutus.

I tried to stave off those pink expectations the second time by preparing myself for another boy, figuring I'd be ready for the inevitable... but pleasantly surprised if a girl came along. That did help me prepare a bit. I've continued to repeat the mantra, "The Lord gives us what we need, and no more than we can handle" and I've read and reread 1 Corinthians 10:13: "And God is faithful; he will not let you be tempted beyond what you can bear." But in the face of four boys in the house, I've been tempted to throw my hands up and shout, "I give up! I just don't understand boys." I'd grown up with one sibling, a sister, so my frame of reference didn't exactly include this boy thing.

Many mothers face this same dilemma. Dan Kindlon and Michael Thompson, in *Raising Cain: Protecting the Emotional Life of Boys,* write that many women are challenged in mothering a son: "They feel they don't understand boys, because they have never actually experienced the world as a boy or they have expectations about boys... which color the way they view their sons."[1] But we moms can't afford not to bridge that gap and connect emotionally with our sons. In his landmark book, *Bringing Up Boys,* Dobson calls the disengagement of parents "the underlying problem plaguing children today."[2]

Today's mothers, though, face an additional challenge from our culture. James and Thomas write in *Wild Things* that it's all too easy to "absorb cultural messages about 'real masculinity'" and push your two- or three-year-old son away emotionally. But, they advise, "A boy needs a connection with his mother all the way through adolescence. Be sensitive about invading your son's privacy, but separating from him prematurely will do him more harm than good."[3]

Even though our blue bundles may seem like alien life-forms to us, we still know that children are blessings and the Lord does give us what He wants us to have. We just have to figure out how to raise and nurture what He has given us. Although ultrasound was available to predict my first son's gender, we decided to be surprised. We were thankful for a healthy child, though I did allow myself to think about the little girl who "might come next"—my first big mistake. But I settled in, with all my expectations and preconceived notions, to enjoy my firstborn. Babies are babies after all, and most moms learn to be happy and thankful for a healthy baby. In the beginning, though, you don't know what you're up against. Those little blue bundles differ greatly from the muddy ten-year-old boy with a frog in his pocket!

... or a Quiet, Calm Baby

The second set of expectations I dealt with related to my sense of peace, quiet, and motherhood. Perhaps the Lord was preparing me for the next twenty years, because the words *peace* and *quiet* usually don't appear in the boy mom vocabulary. I never considered the possibility that Jonathan would be a colicky baby. In my research for this book, I found no statistics indicating that boys are more prone to colic than girls, but Susan Gilbert's *Field Guide to Boys and Girls* does state that, as infants, girls as a group are more alert and more easily consoled. As infants, boys are more easily stressed. In other words, boy babies cry more often when upset and have a harder time calming down.[4] Mothers of boys may be surprised at how much their sons need them.

It never crossed my mind that Jonathan would not be one of those "angel babies"—you know, one who sleeps all the time. Those expectations were shattered. Before long I discovered that he was, indeed, a colicky baby. I remember the afternoon I took him to the doctor and said, "He's slept fifteen minutes today; that's all. Something has to be wrong." The doctor did a few tests and quizzed me, only to pronounce that Jonathan simply had an immature digestive system and most children grew out of it—by three months of age!

Suddenly I flashed back to a chance meeting with a mother and baby months ago. While shopping, I'd stopped to admire her beautiful baby. When I asked how old the baby was, the mom replied, "Three months old, and not a day too soon." Now I knew what she meant.

That first three months with Baby Boy #1 were the longest of my life. He was not at all the angel baby I'd expected. He cried so much, I told my husband, "I'm afraid he's not going to be a happy child." I could just see him frowning the rest of his life. I began to wonder if I could go through this with future babies. At one point, I held Jonathan up in front of my face and asked him, "Don't you want brothers and sisters?"

The doctor told me I was fortunate because Jonathan slept at night and cried all day. What he failed to realize was that I had no help during the day. At night I had help in my husband, but I didn't need it because little Jonathan was snoozing away. When my husband left for work in the morning, the wailing began. On some days I'd meet my husband at the door at five o'clock, thrust Jonathan into his arms, and go for a drive around the block or just take a walk.

Then I'd feel guilty! I had a healthy baby but I spent my time wishing away the hours with him because he just wouldn't stop crying. I began to feel woefully inadequate as a mom. Think about it—Jonathan cried when he was alone with me but was an angel baby when Dad was there.

I knew other mothers who wouldn't take their newborns to the church nursery until they were two or three months. Not me! I had to have a break. I knew the sweet lady there loved babies and had tons of experience, and I had no qualms about leaving him with her. When I asked her about the wisdom of leaving him when he was so fussy, she replied, "Well, honey, he's gonna cry for you or cry for me. Might as well let him cry for me a few hours and give you a break." Those were wise words—precious words to this mom! At least I didn't need to feel guilty about missing church that first three months; I didn't miss a service!

My expectations had crumbled so much, I couldn't even listen to the stories of those moms who had twenty-four-hour angel babies. Such things just could not be true. Babies who ate and drifted off to sleep without a peep? Surely those mothers were lying. Things could not be so idyllic for them. They had no clue what life was like at our house. And how do you share that with friends? "My baby cries so much that I worry he'll never be happy." "I stand at the door at five o'clock and wait to pass him off to my hubby."

I quickly came to the conclusion that the only person who could understand my life those first three months was someone who'd had a similar experience. For some reason, though, those moms don't go around gushing about Early Life with Baby. That's one reason I vowed to share those hard months with other new moms. Maybe that would make them either appreciate those golden hours with their angel baby or sympathize a bit with a friend whose expectations weren't fulfilled.

If your expectations for motherhood include peace and quiet, keep those verses from 2 Samuel handy. You'll need a shield and a refuge. Although Gilbert's research sounds a bit daunting, remember her statement that boy babies, as a group, are easily stressed. That's not to say that all boys are like boys as a group.

But even if you have a quiet, placid little guy now, don't hold too tightly to those expectations for peace and quiet. Babies grow, and toddlerhood ensues.

... That Boys Are Boys

My third big expectation was waiting to trip me up after we added another boy to the picture. When Jonathan hit two years old, we looked at him and said, "Oh, he's not a baby anymore. We need a baby." Several months later, we found we were expecting number two. It was an exciting period. Enough time had elapsed, and Jonathan had turned out to be such a charmer; the memories of colic had faded to oblivion. Besides, hey, we handled that—couldn't we handle just about anything?

We decided against learning this baby's gender; again, we wanted to be surprised. Yes, Daddy did want a little princess, and I thought it would be so much fun to dress a little girl. And like most people, we thought, "A boy and girl would be nice," even though we still intended to add to the family portrait. I tried to prepare myself for a boy. I figured that way I'd be pleasantly surprised if number two was a girl.

But as you already know, another boy it was. We named this one Matthew. He had the same characteristic fair skin and red hair as Jonathan, but the similarities to his brother as an infant ended there. Matthew was the angel baby. It was a whole new world. Now I knew that those other moms weren't lying. Some babies really do eat and sleep and don't cry much at all. That was Baby Boy #2.

I was also pleasantly surprised to learn that two children were, in some ways, easier than one. Baby Matthew had someone to watch, and Jonathan had an instant audience. This proved quite helpful. I could actually get farther than the mailbox before noon, which was unheard of with Baby Boy #1. Of course, my standards for some things likely changed a bit, too. It's incredible how much more quickly one can apply makeup when there's a potential for chaos in the next room.

So far, so good, but the expectation snare was looming. By the time our second son came, we had weathered the terrible twos with the first one. We felt we'd hit upon a successful system of discipline for raising Groves boys. We had read all of Dr. Dobson's books and watched all of his tapes, and I think we felt we had it all figured out. We thought, *Oh, this is the way you handle that. We'll do that with the second child, too.* We knew how to handle rebellion with Boy #1; we'd just apply the same techniques to Boy #2. We expected that he'd react in the same way and all would be well.

We were in for a rude awakening. With Boy #2, we learned there is no magic formula. This wasn't a quick and easy lesson. No, we had to learn it the hard way. Little did we realize that, though our reactions to disobedient behavior remained the same, this child was a different boy. His reactions to us and our discipline would be different. Aye, there's the rub. What to do now?

Looking back, I wonder how I could have been so naïve. I'd taught public school for about nine years, had taught siblings in my classes, and I realized they wouldn't all be the same. I'd taught exceptionally bright students and later their siblings who didn't have the same abilities. But when it came to my own boys, who looked so much the same and were treated in the same way, I just expected their reactions to be the same as well.

There's that word again—*expected.* Maybe part of the problem was a little bit of parental pride. After all, we'd hit upon a successful system and, by golly, it had worked with Boy #1. It was hard to accept that things didn't work the same with Boy #2. A preschool teacher was instrumental in getting something through my thick maternal skull that I should have realized all along. She said to me, "God has made your sons this way on purpose. It's not an accident. As parents, we have to thank God for the children He's given us and ask Him to help us grow them up to be the adults He wants them to be." It finally began to sink in that *different* is not *worse.* It just takes a little more work on Mom's part.

That early lesson became so important later. With a house-ful of kids of the same sex, the temptation is strong to treat them all the same. After all, they're boys. Discovering their dif-ferences—their own individual bent—helped me mother them more effectively. You'll read more about that process in chapter 3, "Intentional Parenting."

The Expectation Trap

No matter what our expectations, our infant sons manage to surprise us. Here are some common elements of the expectation trap. Watch out for them!

- *Regularity.* We may expect regular sleeping and eating times from our infant sons. Some babies seem to be born on a schedule while others defy it. Then there are babies who keep to a schedule for two days—just enough to fool you into thinking you have it all figured out.
- *Activity.* It takes a while to figure out your son's activity level, and that it can change with his age. Gilbert notes that after the age of one, boys spend more time "on the move" than girls do.[5] Although most boys are a bundle of energy, not all are. If you're open to change as you deter-mine your son's activity level, you'll be able to decide how best to structure his active times and sleeping times.
- *Passion.* Some might call this intensity. This is often hard to gauge from an infant, but some little boys seem able to concentrate on one thing, and that ability follows them throughout life. Others are easily distracted. Again, this differs with age, so don't label your son at three months.
- *Responsiveness.* Some infants respond overtly to stimuli, but others are more easygoing. Some boys get more "amped up" in a crowd, while others seem to get wound up in a quiet environment. Be sensitive to your son's responses to different settings.

- *Temperament.* If I had gauged my colicky firstborn by his first three months, I would have believed that he would never smile. He's such a people person today! Don't fall into the trap of labeling your son's temperament or expecting him to turn out one way or another.

So how do we avoid these traps?

Trust Helps Trump Expectations

I'm convinced the answer to the expectation trap lies in trust. If we truly trust the Lord, we know His way is perfect even when we can't see why or how. I couldn't have imagined why He would give me a colicky son, but I had to trust that the Lord knew what He was doing. I've wondered—at tough times—why He gave me four sons. Why not just one little girl to take to all those mother-daughter outings I've had to sit out?

But I've learned I have to let Him be my "refuge and strength, an ever-present help in trouble" (Ps. 46:1). Trusting in Him means staying close to Him. With a houseful of boys, my home does not exactly resemble an ivy-covered chapel. Quiet time has been rare, and reading Scripture can be challenging. Here are some ways I have discovered that can help you look up instead of in, even in a house hopping with boys:

- Try listening to praise music or hymns—that's great for you and the boys.
- Socialization helps, too. When you isolate yourself, you tend to turn inward and focus on your own problems. Get out and take those boys. Take a trip to the library or the park, and enjoy God's creation together.
- Try to get out alone once in a while, even for an hour or two. Call a friend and indulge in some girl talk. E-mail someone supportive.
- Don't miss opportunities to worship.

Remember, expectations blind us to our blessings. It took me a couple more boys to learn that.

Discarding Expectations

As Boys #3 and #4 came along, I became convinced that expectations were, indeed, a trap. I didn't shed them without a struggle, but they had to go. Our third son, Andrew, was due on New Year's Day, but he decided to make his debut on, of all days, Christmas Eve. I had the holiday all planned, and I didn't expect this. I remember my tearful words before we left for the hospital: "I really didn't want to have a Christmas baby," to which my husband nervously answered, "Honey, I don't think we have much choice here, so let's just go." Then three years later our fourth son, Benjamin, made an unexpected and dramatic debut via C-section—after I'd had natural deliveries with the first three. That really upset my apple cart, but this time it was my mother's wise words that helped me pitch my expectations. She said, "Honey, you're just paying a few extra weeks of recovery in return for a healthy boy."

Discarding expectations allowed me to grow beyond my own fixed ideas and see what God, in His wisdom, had for me. In the raising of our four sons, I've discarded expectations time and again. Our first son was quite compliant to authority, a preschool dream. Matthew, on the other hand, had a bit more stubborn nature. Imagine my dismay when I arrived to pick Matthew up from preschool one day. He'd been playing in a big box, and the teacher had called him to Circle Time several times. The last time she encouraged him to do the right thing by saying, "We need to choose to obey." Matthew calmly and matter-of-factly replied, "I choose to disobey." I was appalled, certain that he'd be a juvenile delinquent—then his principal reminded me that stubbornness isn't always a bad quality. She added, though, that we must teach our children to be stubborn for the right things, a lesson that has served me well as my boys have grown.

Discarding expectations is hard, but it results in growth for our sons, for us as moms, and for our relationships with our sons. Our boys need to know that even if much in the rest of their lives is performance-based, our love isn't. We love them because they are ours and they were crafted by the Father and given to us as gifts. As we endeavor to raise our boys to be godly men, we need them to see their uniqueness and their potential. If they're taught to be cookie-cutter boys who fit neatly within Mom's expectations, they'll never find out who they really are and what God's unique purpose for them is.

Beyond My Expectations

As the boys grew and multiplied, so did the noise and the activity—beyond my expectations. Unless you had brothers, you don't really expect the racket, the constant motion, the physicality that comes with a combination of boys. And even if you did grow up around brothers, you likely weren't in charge of them. But noise and activity come with the territory, so one of a boy mom's first lessons is to relinquish those expectations and free ourselves to look at life from a different perspective—a boy's perspective. *What if… I could climb from the top of that tree to the roof of the house? What if… I buried ants in mud; would they suffocate? What if… I could slice a banana with the ceiling fan?*

Most boys will not only ask these questions, they'll experiment to see if they can answer them. In *Wild Things*, James and Thomas discuss the differences between the mind of a boy and the mind of a girl. They note that on the whole, boys tend to be

- *spatial instead of relational.* They understand the lay of the land, for example, and how things are connected.
- *aware of objects instead of faces.* They're more attracted to objects than they are to people.
- *action-oriented instead of process-oriented.* They're oriented to movement rather than to emotions.[6]

You see the differences. Moms relate to faces and emotions; our boys generally relate to things and movement. Armed with this understanding, it may be a little easier to determine why that little boy did what he did. At the very least, being aware of the general differences can make a mom aware that she needs to step back and assess her son through different eyes.

Chaos, Creativity, and Control

My best description of a household of multiple boys would be this: controlled chaos and creativity. Boys do have to be allowed to explore, to try the boundaries, to create—but with controls. All children need creative outlets, but with a boy's penchant for movement and his innate desire to figure out the process (*What makes that toaster glow?*), controls are imperative. I'm not saying that chaos is preferred or necessary; it's simply a foregone conclusion with multiple boys. Perhaps *chaos* isn't exactly the right word. Maybe the word *upheaval* is more accurate. Upheaval can indicate anything from change to explosion... and both are likely in a household of boys. *Upheaval* and *change* are unsettling words for most moms. We prefer *predictable* and *manageable*.

Boys can be very manageable if you sit them in front of the mesmerizing television all day. But eventually you have to turn it off—and then you pay for it... at bed time and later in life. Boys need to be able to entertain themselves safely, and they need to exercise creativity to do that. Provide them with toys that will foster creativity:

- *Manipulative toys.* Your first purchase for your sons should be blocks. Boys need tactile toys, and they love things they can take apart and sometimes even put back together. Toys that teach cause and effect are important— turn this, and that pops out; push this, and something else happens. Remember, they're process-oriented and love movement.

- *Books.* Don't wait until your boys can read to provide books. Start them with cloth and plastic books when they're infants. Look for books with pull tabs and doors that open, or books shaped like trucks with wheels. Try to appeal to what boys innately adore in a creative, interactive way. Reading is a challenge for many boys later, so use these early years to engender a love for books and stories.

What about control? Some moms do more controlling than anything else. If you're guilty of that, you may need to sit back, sit on your hands if necessary, and let your boy try things on his own. You should be present, however, even if you seem to be in the background. Even though my sons are pretty much grown up, I still put on my makeup at the mirror in the front hall. That started when there were two little boys in the den; I could keep an eye and ear on them more easily from that vantage point. When we looked for a house, we planned for the family room to be for the boys, and I wanted an adjoining kitchen. I figured I would be spending most of my time in the kitchen, and I could be there while keeping an eye on the boys. You're the mom, and some control is obviously necessary.

As for creativity, it can be messy—I won't deny that. But keeping boys occupied and productive is worth the mess, at least temporarily. That's why I suggest you keep a few things around for the boys:

- String
- Sticks
- Boxes
- An "art box" full of markers, stickers, paints, and so forth

You have to be careful, of course, and age-appropriate with these things. If you happen to have a boys-plus household, your girls will enjoy creating as well. Whether they work together or on separate projects, a creative outlet will be good for sons as well as daughters.

My boys still remember some of the masterpieces they crafted from such materials—boxes taped together to build a robot, string used as an imaginary dog (or lion) leash, sticks laid end to end and parallel to form a highway... and they all tell the story of the huge appliance box that served as a fort, a pirate ship, a skyscraper. The day it fell apart in the rain was perhaps the most fun, as they slid down a hill on the leftover pieces.

A Healthy Expectation

Although expectations can be a trap, there is one expectation you should hold on to: Greet each new day with the expectation that it will be a wild ride. Then you'll be ready for anything! This is an essential piece of advice for the mothers of multiple boys. If for some reason things are calm at day's end, you'll simply be pleasantly surprised.

2

The Magnet Syndrome (aka Sibling Rivalry)

A friend loves at all times,
and a brother is born for adversity.

PROVERBS 17:17

There are two ways to look at Proverbs 17:17. Usually it's interpreted that a brother is always there, a support and help, in times of adversity. Sometimes, however, it seems that a brother is born *for* adversity. When you have two or more boys, there are days when it seems brothers are born for one reason—to annoy one another. Girls do the same to each other, and sibling rivalry occurs between a brother and a sister, but when a family has multiple boys, a certain dynamic is created.

My husband calls it the Magnet Syndrome. Have you ever taken a pair of magnets and placed them close together? Obviously, they attract. But that's not all. If you turn the magnets over, they repel. That's what it's like so many times with multiple boys—they attract, they repel. Hands on, hands off. They wrestle, they hang on, they push away. It's inevitable—something to do with the laws of nature. I see it even in my high school classroom. A boy walks by another to sharpen a pencil, and he *has* to reach out and touch another boy—step on his foot, bop him on the head, slap him on the shoulder. And they think it's hilarious when you tell them to keep their hands off each other. Does it happen with girls? No! Sure, girls touch, but they hold hands and braid hair. Boys push, step on, and bop. It's part of that guy thing—the Magnet Syndrome.

Divide and Conquer

The Magnet Syndrome isn't always a bad thing, but with the physicality of two or three boys, things can quickly turn crazy. Susan Gilbert cites the results of studies that show boys are most active when they're with other boys.[1] If you have multiple boys, that's pretty much all the time. The best thing a mom can do is just be aware of the possibility for craziness—and be ready to intervene if necessary. At times it's best just to separate them. Get one involved in another activity elsewhere, but don't let on why, of course. That will certainly defeat the purpose. If they know Mom doesn't want them together, their prime objective will become getting back together.

You have to creatively present alternatives that will seem appealing. In their toddler and preschool years, bath time was great fun for my boys. They entered the tub kingdom armed with boats, seaplanes, little people, and countless butter tubs that they could pour from. When it was time to enact the separatist philosophy, many times I'd suggest that one of the boys play in the tub—no matter what time of day. Once one was in the tub, I could supervise while involving the other in some activity in the hallway right outside the bathroom door and— mission accomplished—separation was successfully achieved. In the midst of new play, the conflict was soon forgotten.

Another method that can work when boys are young is changing their focus. Try to unite them by having them challenge Mom at something. "Let's see if you two can pick up those blocks faster than Mom can collect the cars." Or "Let's take a big piece of paper and make a 'Welcome home from work' card for Daddy. Here's the middle. Pete, you take this side and Dan will take that side. Let's fill up the card with pictures." If you can get them to work together on something, even momentarily, the focus can change.

Maybe it's just time for a new activity. Sometimes their energies just need to be channeled a bit. Quick and creative thinking on Mom's part can get them back on track.

Or maybe you just need to join in the fun. It could be that both boys need more "Mom time." It's so easy to get caught up in the things that need to be done around the house and forget to be involved with the boys. Stop and think—is there anything the boys could help you with? If you can present sorting laundry as fun or challenging or a "big-boy" job, you may win them over. Maybe those plastic containers need to be sorted by size so they'll all fit in the kitchen cabinet. (*Or maybe they'd make a great tower…*) You may have to lower your standards a bit and possibly do some re-sorting later but, for the moment at least, you've restored peace and helped the boys gain a sense of accomplishment and teamwork.

Don't Hurt Your Brother

Sibling rivalry and sparring brothers also surface when the boys are as tall as you are. And the potential for brother-upon-brother damage unfortunately increases as they grow. That's why it's important to lay the groundwork early on the no-hurting policy. It's always been my contention that no one should mistreat my children—not even another one of my children. *Especially,* in fact, not another one of my children. Psalm 133:1 reminds us, "How good and pleasant it is when brothers live together in unity!" I've always wanted my boys to love and stand up for one another, and as soon as I had my first two boys I vowed that they would not hit one another. They may have pushed from time to time and they may have come awfully close to socking one another—and the last chapter is still not written on that yet. But I've done my best to make sure they don't engage in daily slugfests. "You don't hit your brother" has always been taken for granted in our house. It was verbalized early and often and reinforced repeatedly.

A more accurate admonition would be "You don't hurt your brother." That covers not only physical but emotional abuse. If we want to raise boys who value home, it must be a place of safety. If an adolescent is to value family above peer concerns, home should be a haven, a place of comfort and stability. If a boy feels he'll be ridiculed at home but praised by his peers, whose value system will he prize? The world can be a hard place, especially for boys who may have a tough time expressing their feelings. Home should be the place where they can express their concerns and fears and talk things out. If they grow up being the target of sarcasm and criticism at home, how can we expect them to develop into godly young men of compassion and promise?

And as I tell my boys, they're brothers forever. Someday they'll be dads and after that, granddads. They'll likely have families of their own and form new friendships, but they'll always be brothers. So just as you don't hit your brother, you don't call your brother names or try to make him feel like he's not worthy. I often asked, "How would you feel if your brother did that to you?" We've all heard that boys don't like to talk about their feelings, but starting this early will make it easier for them. And, hopefully, you'll succeed in helping them to think about how their words and actions affect others.

... or Your Sister

In the boys-plus household—the family with at least one sister in the mix—the "don't hurt your brother" admonition takes on another dimension. I know a mom who has a mixture of sons and daughters, and she's noticed a meaner spirit in the bickering between the sexes. This mom says that when a brother verbally spars with his sister, their words seem more pointed and hurtful. The boys know they can't hit a sister, so they wound them as deeply as they can with words.

And a special warning to the mom in the boys-plus household: be careful not to buy into "boys will be boys." If a son is particularly insensitive when sparring with his sister, fight the urge to let the issue go with, "Well, he just doesn't understand how that hurts you." Hold him accountable for what he says and does, and use the conflict to open the window a bit on his sister's emotions. Watch out for Sister as well. Make sure she's not crying wolf, claiming a wounded spirit just to get you to intervene.

Guide your son and daughter in settling their own conflicts, and sit back and watch and listen as it happens. (For more on the boys-plus household, see the end of this chapter.)

Who Comes Out on Top?

The boys' playful wrestling can be just that—a fun session of roughhousing. But sibling rivalry can often be what leads to the Magnet Syndrome, and it often has another purpose—to see who comes out on top. The mom of multiple boys recognizes this motive at ages two and four, and even ten years later. With multiple boys, the question surfaces again and again—who *will* come out on top? Whether it's a physical challenge, a verbal sparring match, a trivia contest, or simply the correct pronunciation of a word, its goal is the same: to see who will come out on top this time.

This brings up the search for what I call the "delicate balance." A mom wants to raise her boys to be competitive in a healthy way. She wants them to acquire leadership qualities. Does that mean she encourages such sparring between brothers and rewards the winner? That will only increase feelings of sibling rivalry. We have to teach our boys early and often to consider their motivation. "Why do you need to convince Bobby that you say it this way and not that way?" "How important is it to always win?" "Have you thought about how other people feel when you act that way?" We moms need to talk about such things with our boys.

In one particular elementary school playground incident, one of my sons was convinced he was right about some fact. He badgered a little girl with that information until she cried. He was technically right about the fact in question, but we had a discussion about letting go and simply having confidence in the fact that you're right. I told him, "You may be right about something, but if you have to make someone cry to convince them, that's not right." That may sound like a sophisticated concept, but a grade school child can easily understand it when it's put in context for him and his life.

Many times a two-year-old brother will argue that the sky is green before he has his colors straight, or he'll hold up two fingers, insisting it's five. You can first give him the facts, but after a point, it does no good to argue with his stubborn "two-ness" and you simply have to let it go, knowing you're right. Our sons need to learn this lesson as well. Someday the two-year-old will admit the sky is blue, although I'm sure he'll deny he ever argued differently.

We moms of multiple boys have a delicate balance to maintain. We need to encourage leadership and independent thinking, but at the same time, we must balance that with lessons about excessive pride, healthy self-confidence, and understanding others.

Who Takes the Lead?

One of the best ways to develop leadership in all of your boys is to give everyone a chance to lead at something. Your sons' feelings of sibling rivalry can be replaced with a sense of leadership and accomplishment when each is given a chance to lead or excel. In our family, there were certain things only the oldest could do, simply because he was old enough or tall enough or strong enough. But Mom had to make opportunities for others to take the lead in other areas. Look for every opportunity to give responsibility to all of your boys.

- Give your boys age-appropriate chores or duties in the household, and rotate those chores among the boys so that all of them get a chance at some responsibility. Thank them for fulfilling those responsibilities and let them know they're helping the family.
- When you're taking a walk, vary who gets to walk first or who gets to push the baby stroller. Teach them to take

turns in the small things, to be leaders, and to know how to yield leadership.

- Do your best to be fair. Ask your husband to observe and to tell you if he thinks you're spreading the privileges and responsibilities equally. Sometimes a different perspective can shed light on something you haven't perceived.

- Realize there are times when it's best not to settle a quarrel. Sometimes the argument has grown so that it has become "Who will win this one?" Sometimes the son who is technically right has an attitude that's all wrong. Other cases just require a cooling-off period—"Boys, go to separate rooms while you think about what you did and said." After some time alone, my boys usually came up with what was right and wrong about the altercation, and that enabled me to use it as a teaching moment. If I'd responded in the heat of the moment, nothing would have been gained.

- Deliberately choose activities that showcase all of your boys' abilities. Maybe Jack never wants to skate because he's not as steady on his feet as his younger brother, but he always wins at basketball. Get the whole crew out there skating as well as shooting hoops, so the younger one can achieve some success as well. To this day, our youngest has a Monopoly strategy that puts the others under the table. They complain, but it's great to see him beat the brother who's nine years older!

Each son will know he is special if he isn't excluded from leadership. As each learns to lead, the others learn how to follow. Pretty soon, you'll have established a foundation for teamwork among your boys. Teamwork results in a spirit of unity, "so that with one heart and mouth you may glorify the God and Father of our Lord Jesus Christ" (Rom. 15:6).

Who Gets the Attention?

Sibling rivalry often occurs because someone feels slighted. Frank J. Sulloway writes in *Born to Rebel* that "siblings employ strategies aimed at maximizing parental investment."[2] Sometimes a son is begging you to take sides, to show your investment in him over his brother. Why does that happen? Right or not, one son feels he's not getting the attention or support that someone else is getting. That's hard to see in the heat of the moment when Brandon is whaling on Joey, but if you stop and think about it, you can usually see some reason behind it. Sometimes all that's needed is a little attention. It's hard to give one-on-one attention when you have multiple boys, but a little attention can go a long way.

Sometimes just talking about the offense can be helpful. Try to get the offending son off by himself in a relaxed setting and ask him why he's been taking Tommy's toys or why he says mean things to Joe. When his brothers aren't there, he'll likely open up. You may find out something is going on that you didn't expect. He could be retaliating for something that you aren't even aware of. Handling conflicts this way enables boys to see that getting to the root of a problem is more helpful than just reacting. Instead of solving the momentary conflict with a shove, they can actually talk things out and reach a solution. Here are some hints for dealing with each son:

- Talk with each son alone, then with the sons together. You may need to institute a cooling-off period before you sit down to talk. Give them time to think about what just happened.
- Stop what you're doing and give your full attention to each son. I know you have a thousand things to do, but this time will pay off in the long run by teaching conflict resolution.
- Use your eyes and ears. Look your son in the eye and listen closely. Don't finish his sentences or anticipate where

he's going with his explanation. Let him know you really care about what he's saying and how he feels.

- Let him verbalize his feelings. Even if they're not valid ("You like Thomas better!"), that doesn't negate the fact that he feels that way. If you listen closely without preconceived notions, his emotions will give you valuable insight into his behavior.

In this process, you may even find out something about yourself and your mothering style that needs a little repair.

The Battleground as a Training Ground

Realize that bouts of sibling rivalry are teachable moments—for you and for your sons. If correctly handled, those moments will teach your boys valuable lessons about conflict management, and you will learn more about your sons and what really drives them. If you use these times of conflict to get to the root of the discord and find out what your sons are really thinking, you'll obviously understand them better. So rather than glossing over the problems with a "punish and forget" attitude, take time to ask the questions that will reveal the root of the problem.

And perhaps you, as a mom, have lessons to learn in conflict management, too. Maybe you've always just responded in the heat of the moment, coming down quickly on one side or the other, assuming you knew who had to be the culprit. Perhaps that's the way you grew up, and no one modeled effective conflict resolution for you. There's hope. Here are some hints:

- Ask the Lord to reveal to you your inadequacies in managing conflict.
- Look for help in the Scriptures. Remember, "For everything that was written in the past was written to teach us, so that through endurance and the encouragement of the Scriptures we might have hope" (Rom. 15:4).

- Pray for patience and guidance in dealing with your boys. If your witness as a mom has been less than stellar, take your shortcomings to the Lord, remembering to "humble yourselves, therefore, under God's mighty hand, that he may lift you up in due time" (1 Peter 5:6).
- Even in the heat of the moment, after perhaps shouting, "BOYS!" say in your heart, "Father, help me with this ..."
- Pray with your sons, even sharing your conflicts with the Lord. At the end of the day, thank Him for helping you work through the conflicts. Remember that "no discipline seems pleasant at the time, but painful. Later on, however, it produces a harvest of righteousness and peace for those who have been trained by it" (Heb. 12:11).
- Look back at the four previous hints for dealing with your son. Take a deep breath, breathe a prayer, and use those hints instead of yelling and threatening and saying things you'll wish you hadn't.

And how do the boys learn from this? If you can effectively model conflict resolution, they'll learn by example. Don't worry if you've blown it up to this point. It's beneficial for them to see you working to improve your own responses to stressful situations. If they notice the before-and-after difference in you, they may realize it's much more satisfying and effective to talk things through and try to understand one another.

As the boys get older and when it's safe, turn them loose to solve conflicts on their own. I'd still stay close, depending on their ages, their proclivities, and the heatedness of their conflict, but let them see what they can do to move closer together. The proof of the pudding is not that you can help resolve conflict; it's that your sons ultimately learn how to do it on their own. Realize that this may take awhile, and you may not see the fruits of your efforts... but isn't that what much of mothering is about? We plant the seeds and water them, then we pray and wait. And we water a little bit more, and we plant some more seeds, and we water some more... then we dump fertilizer on the ground ... Sometimes we have to remind ourselves of Galatians 6:9: "Let us not become weary in doing good, for at the proper time we will reap a harvest if we do not give up." Mothering is a big job, and the rewards usually don't come quickly. We often don't see the results of all our hard work and prayer, but we have to trust God to bring forth the fruit in His season. All that we do as mothers goes into shaping the men our sons will be, so keep watering that ground.

Mom's Word Goes

It probably goes without saying that in the mom-son triangle (or square or pentagon) of multiple boys, Mom's word goes. I've devoted much time to "talking about talking" in this chapter—questioning, attempting to understand. But use some discretion, Mom, because at times you may have to shut down dangerous or mean behavior without a lot of discussion—at least initially. And remember, your one-on-one time isn't an opportunity for your son to wheedle and convince and wear you down. You and Dad have set certain rules in the household (see appendix A for "Dad's Part in All of This"), and it's up to you to do your part to hold the boys accountable. But it doesn't hurt to debrief a bit—to talk with them about what happened, why it was wrong, and why it happened. Avoid lecturing, but ask questions and let the boys respond, and guide them to understanding. That's what makes the whole conflict a learning experience. If your boys don't learn from something, whatever punishment has been imposed won't matter.

You should strike while the iron is hot—don't wait for Dad to get home! Granted, some things should be dealt with on a father-son level. But that doesn't stop you from stopping the misbehavior. You can at least begin to understand what has happened and then let Dad follow through, if that seems more appropriate.

Love Covers a Multitude of Sons

You may be asking, "Can't we just avoid this whole sibling rivalry thing?" T. Berry Brazelton, M.D., writes, "Don't expect their conflict to go away. Ever."[3] Any mother of multiple children will tell you that it's just not possible to totally avoid sibling rivalry. Here are some hints, however, for minimizing it:

- Consider each of your boys as unique individuals. Get rid of any preconceived notions you may have about who in the family they're like or what they'll grow up to do. Give each son the freedom to be his own boy. It's fine if one likes music and another likes the great outdoors—and it's fine if they both love the great outdoors. There's room in the family for more than one outdoorsman, if that's their bent. Just don't force them to be what they're not, maybe to fulfill some long-lost dream of yours.

- If your sons are vastly different from each other or from you, celebrate that. How boring life would be if we were all alike! Our differences sometimes take getting used to, but remember that our differences are evidence of God's creativity.

- Be positive. Even if your son is negative about something he can't do, point out something he's really good at. Make a habit of telling your sons, "I like it when you..." or "You do such a good job at..." It's important to be truthful but hopeful. Some abilities will come later in life, and some are just waiting to be discovered.

- If your son makes a mistake, don't humiliate him or say, "What did you do this time?" Be sure he understands the error of his ways, but then help him, don't demean him. Whether he's knocked over his toddler brother's tower or wrecked the family car, he needs help.

- Love him—unconditionally. When he succeeds, when he fails, when he shines, when he falls—love him unconditionally. You may not love what he does, but make sure he knows you still love *him*. And perhaps it's because you love him that you don't love what he does, because your ultimate desire is for him to be happy and healthy and in favor with God and man. Be sure he knows, even in the worst of times, that you love him.

Benefits for the Boys-Plus Household

If there's a girl or two in your house of multiple boys, you may have some unique concerns, but researchers cite the benefits of such a mix. Each family has its own dilemmas, but the author of *Brothers and Sisters: How They Shape Our Lives* writes of the problems that may face "tilted families"—that is, families with all boys or all girls. Research suggests these families may struggle with behavior control and may register a sense of loss because there are not children of both sexes.[4] Not so for the boys-plus family. Since you have a smattering of pink and blue in your household, your children have the opportunity to see how the other half lives. Just this week, I was talking with a friend who has a daughter between her two sons. She explained to me that she felt her daughter really "got" boys since she had one on either side.

Most of us would admit that women have a civilizing influence on the opposite sex, and Susan Gilbert has written about research that supports this. She quotes an educational professional with more than three decades of experience in teaching young children: "The presence of girls seems to help with the process [of boys' adjustment to preschool], which is one reason why some teachers make a policy of having equal numbers of boys and girls in each class. Boys and girls learn by watching each other."[5] As boys watch the school behavior of girls, they learn about the classroom. Another teacher reports seeing girls branching out physically and becoming more active as they associate with boys. Even if your children are not in the classroom together, consider the benefits of their constant interaction. Your household is an environment in which your sons are exposed to at least one more female creature besides you. That's bound to give them a clearer daily view of how to live among the opposite sex than they'd get in my house of five males, one female.

Brothers and sisters can help one another, too, in balancing their emotional reactions. Since many boys tend to hold in their feelings and girls often embrace them, the opportunities for lessons are clear. Both boys and girls need balance in this area. If brothers can see the value of expressing emotion, and sisters can learn to leave them behind at times—letting things go instead of dwelling on them—they'll face life with valuable skills gleaned from one another. They can begin to get a sense of what makes the other sex tick, they can begin to see what it means to grow up as a male or female, and they can understand that both have fears and weaknesses that are not so different.

Having a younger sister or two gives brothers a chance to express their protectiveness and devotion. Who hasn't heard stories of an older, protective brother always looking out for his little sister? (I always wished for brothers ... my mother says I finally got my due with four sons.) The author of *Mixed Feelings: Love, Hate, Rivalry, and Reconciliation Among Brothers and Sisters* recalls listening to tapes of interviews with adult siblings. The interviewees showed such similarity about a big brother's being there for his little sister, she felt she was listening to the story of one life.[6] An older brother's protectiveness can give a sister a sense of worth and value and make her feel secure.

Sisters amidst a sea of brothers have their own unique function, as well, which they often perform into adulthood. In one study of sibling relationships of those over sixty, both males and females named a sister as the one to whom they felt the closest. Sisters are often called "kin keepers," keeping family ties alive and strong.[7] Long after Mom and Dad are gone, the sister of the bunch will likely be the one who provides the glue for your sons.

A sister's love and support can be similar to Mom's, but it sometimes comes with fewer strings attached. While Mom's advice comes from a place of authority, a sister's advice can be offered without condemnation or judgment.

One caution to mothers of a bunch of boys with a girl sandwiched in: it's easy for a girl to feel trivialized among a bunch of boys, so take seriously her reaction to the boys' teasing. It will be easy for them to band together against the alien of the bunch, whether she's younger or older. Don't buy into the "boys will be boys" myth. Teach your sons to treat their sister with respect. (You'll find more hints on engendering respect in chapter 8, "Growing Respect.") If they learn to respect their sister, they'll grow into men who are more attuned to a woman's interests and feelings, thanks to being sensitized to them over the years.

Brothers Are for Keeps

"A friend loves at all times, and a brother is born for adversity" (Prov. 17:17). A mom's hope is that, when all is said and done, the brothers will be there for one another at all times, even in adversity. That's possible if they understand the value of both leadership and teamwork. My boys are like most guys—they don't have an overabundance of good male friends. They have one or two close friends, but even those have been hard to find. In retrospect, I think that might be because they have such high expectations for friendship. I've had to remind them that no matter how close your friends are, they won't be as close as your brothers. And what a great thing that is!

3

Intentional Parenting

Are not five sparrows sold for two pennies? Yet not one of them is forgotten by God. Indeed, the very hairs of your head are all numbered. Don't be afraid; you are worth more than many sparrows.

LUKE 12:6-7

Building a band of brothers is a challenge. Acknowledging what makes each son unique as the brotherhood develops takes intentional parenting. What, you may ask, is intentional parenting? It's parenting on purpose, with intent. When you have multiple sons, your intent needs to be to know each one individually. Once you begin to understand the differences between your boys, you need to deal with those differences. That becomes more difficult as the number of boys increases.

When we added the third son, Andrew, to our mix, I noticed a big change. The newborn wasn't the challenge—it was handling the rest of the household and mothering three at once. I'd had a three-year-old and a baby before, but I hadn't had an elementary school child in addition to those. And this time, Jonathan was in first grade, which meant homework and more of a schedule and structure. That, added to caring for a three-year-old and an infant, was a challenge. Jonathan was very self-motivated and loved school, but every child needs a bit of help and encouragement with homework. This was our first real school experience, and we wanted Jonathan to do well. As the typical firstborn, he wanted to achieve as well, so we immersed ourselves in first-grade life.

You can probably guess the problem that emerged. On the one hand, much effort was being expended toward first-grade success; on the other, much time and effort was required in the care of a newborn. That left us with the typical middle-child syndrome. Matthew was three—active, imaginative, and energetic. It was too easy to let him entertain himself. More than once, I was led by his small hand from what I was doing to what he was doing. A middle child has his own particular bugaboos—he will forever be in the middle. He's not the big guy—the oldest who gets to drive first—and he's not the cute baby who gets a lot of attention. At least with four boys now, my middle one has company, but when there were three, he didn't. He was between the first-grade star and the cute baby. A tough place to be.

A Rude Awakening

One particular incident convinced me that I needed to be more intentional about my parenting. When Matthew was about three and a half, I discovered a picture I'd taken of the two oldest boys watching television, and I noticed that Matthew had his head tilted down and was squinting up at the TV. I started to watch more carefully when he was in front of things and noticed the same behavior. We took him to a pediatric ophthalmologist and discovered that, indeed, he needed glasses. I agonized in typical mother-like fashion, "How long has this been going on? Poor child! He probably hasn't been able to see for months, and I've been too busy with a first-grader and a baby to notice!" My mother wisely said, "Honey, just be thankful this is something that can be so easily fixed." She was right, of course.

But there were other worries. Would he like the glasses? Would he keep them on? I envisioned a constant battle. The doctor assured me that Matthew would wear the glasses because he'd be able to see so well. And the doctor was right! Matthew's glasses suffered some breakage of course—we had the Magnet Syndrome to deal with. We found an optician, though, who had a "child plan," which included a few extra dollars for insurance. We visited them frequently to bend frames back into place and even for a number of replacements. We took the insurance to the limit. And after all the agonizing I'd done, someone asked if I'd gotten those glasses just to make him look cute. I couldn't believe it! But when it was all said and done, I learned quite a lesson about being intentional and being tuned in to each of my sons.

To Be an Intentional Mom, You Have to Be . . . Well, *Intentional*

I quickly learned that intentional parenting takes not only time but effort and involvement. At the beginning of the parenting marathon, most parents expect to expend time and effort and involve themselves with their children. But modern culture is so fast-paced, crowding us with stuff to distract us, it's easy to get caught up in the swirl and get sidetracked from parenting.

We can even think we're spending enough time with our kids while our sons perceive it differently. Meg Meeker, M.D., reports in *Boys Should Be Boys* the results of one study: 21 percent of children said they needed more time with their parents. When the parents of these kids were surveyed, however, only 8 percent felt they needed more time with their children.[1] If we intend to parent on purpose, we need constantly to remind ourselves of several things:

- *Priorities.* An intentional mom puts parenting in the forefront.
- *Stereotypes.* The common "boy" stereotype can be a real pitfall for the mother of multiple boys. Boys are seen as able, strong creatures who don't need any help from Mom. Nothing could be further from the truth.
- *Differences.* Differences can be helpful. Most moms see boys as so different from ourselves that we can get caught up in those differences, not seeing beyond them or figuring out how to use those differences. In reality, it's Mom's different perspective that can help boys become strong, able young men.

It seems easy for Mom to let boys go their own way simply because they are boys. If we do that, however, we sacrifice the opportunity for the nurturing that leads to a close mother-son relationship full of love and trust. In *Bringing Up Boys*, Dobson writes about the need for nurturing, something he calls "playing offense." Dobson contends that parents need to "play defense on behalf of their sons—that is, as they protect their boys from immoral and dangerous enticements. But that's not enough. Parents also need to play offense—to capitalize on the impressionable years of childhood by instilling in their sons the antecedents of character."[2]

Look at the football metaphor in a mother's terms: when we play defense, we're the mother hen in protection mode; to play offense, we have to be intentional about both teaching our sons and teaming up with them to move them forward into the outside world. A workable formula that will help you parent your boys on purpose consists of four elements: nurture them physically, inspire them intellectually, cultivate them socially, and nourish them spiritually.

Nurture Them Physically

Don't buy into the notion that boys don't need physical nurturing. Boys need hugs just as much as girls do. How do you nurture them physically across the ages?

- When they're infants, be sure you hug and hold and swaddle your sons.
- As toddlers, they need to be praised with hugs, and kissed good night.
- As they grow, be aware of their changing needs. Some boys at ten or twelve feel they're too big for a kiss from Mom in public. Respect that and don't embarrass him, but do affirm him with a touch, at least at home. A quick squeeze across the shoulders, a kiss on the cheek, a warm hug tells your son that you love him, even if he feels stiff as cardboard in your arms.

We communicate love to our sons through touch before they can understand a word we say. Christ touched to heal; Thomas touched and believed. Touch matters. Touch communicates across the ages. The authors of *Raising Cain* remind us that our sons need the caring touch that mothers provide. As one of the few women who can give a boy emotional comfort through touch in a nonsexual context, we moms have a big responsibility. As Kindlon and Thompson write, "Boys need to experience that physical tenderness if they are to speak the language later. Otherwise we leave their touch training to football coaches [and] wrestling opponents."[3]

Do remember to treat each son as an individual. My firstborn was in my sophomore English class at school, and he never left the classroom without giving me a kiss on the cheek. The next son would leave with a smile and "See ya, Mom—good class today." The third always took time to say goodbye and might give me a hug from time to time, and the fourth is proud of me but is easily embarrassed by me. I could easily embarrass Benjamin with a hug in front of everyone, but I tend to resist the temptation and save the hug for home. Remember that your boys are all different, but they all need an affirming touch at one time or another.

Another important way to nurture your son physically is by providing him times of rest. Believe it or not, boys need rest. They have to recharge sometime! Don't make the mistake of letting your boy go until he falls over. Regular times of rest and relaxation serve to balance his inbred sense of activity.

Maybe your toddler son won't nap. You can at least insist on a time of rest for him—and you. Set guidelines for quiet time. Give him books, play soothing music, and insist that he stay on his bed for the duration. Just because they're boys doesn't mean they can't learn to appreciate quiet. Too many children today are conditioned to be entertained every moment of every day, often by electronic devices. Whether or not they believe it, they will encounter times in their lives when there is no TV or video game to distract, and they'll need to call upon their own resources. Teaching them to relax quietly when they're small will help them when they find themselves in such situations.

So much can be learned from times of rest. When your mind isn't preoccupied by someone or something, it's free to be creative. We've always taken long road trips in the summer—partially because flying six people was cost-prohibitive. So the boys learned early how to occupy themselves. (See chapter 10, "A Word from the Boys," for their take on family vacations.) There was no DVD player in the car, but there were books and games and toy soldiers—and brothers! Mom's little "trip surprises" helped too—small, inexpensive games or puzzle books or toy cars that gave them something to look forward to. To this day, we all enjoy a long drive in the car because it gives us the opportunity to talk, to listen, to read, and just to think. If you constantly bombard boys with stimuli, they'll never have the opportunity to realize the joys of a bit of quiet.

One obvious way to nurture your boys physically is to feed them! One of my sons is so appreciative of food that he's a joy to cook for. He never leaves the table without thanking me or commenting positively on some aspect of the dinner. Another son seems to open up across the table. You can be one-on-one with him in the car and get no conversation, but sit alone with him at a table of food and you get dialogue. And it's important to really *nurture* them with food, not just fill them up. Teach them to eat healthy food. Sugar, preservatives, and boys can be a dangerous combination!

We can also be intentional about food by getting to know the likes and dislikes of our sons, catering to each from time to time. For birthday dinners in our home, in addition to gathering gifts and the cake, Mom cooks up the birthday boy's favorite dish. As the boys have grown and gone off to college, they often find their favorites on the menu when they're back for a visit. It's a small thing, but it communicates love.

Inspire Them Intellectually

Our sons won't all be scholars and some may struggle in school, but that doesn't mean you should neglect their intellect.

Children have natural curiosity that can be fostered, and that curiosity can lead to learning. You'll be successful if you can provide your boys with a love for learning. That desire may be squelched in some educational environments, but if it's instilled early, it will stay with your son. When he finds his niche and the freedom to pursue it at some point in life, he'll still have the natural curiosity that will lead him to learn all there is to learn about what he loves.

As Christian parents, we desire to lead our boys to an understanding of their Creator and His love for them. That's a lifetime pursuit, and fostering our sons' intellect and curiosity now can lead to their later search for insight and understanding. Proverbs 2:1–5 recalls the godly search for wisdom that we desire for our sons: "My son, if you accept my words and store up my commands within you, turning your ear to wisdom and applying your heart to understanding, and if you call out for insight and cry aloud for understanding, and if you look for it as for silver and search for it as for hidden treasure, then you will understand the fear of the LORD and find the knowledge of God." Our efforts to nurture our sons intellectually can lead not only to a recitation of the ABCs, but to the discovery of wisdom and insight. What a gift to give our sons!

The best way to inspire your son intellectually is to foster a love for learning. Here are some hints:

- *Talk.* Even before your boy is old enough to speak, talk to him about what you're doing. Narrate that sandwich you're making or talk about whose clothes you're folding. This will increase his verbal and listening skills, and once he's old enough, he'll be asking you questions.
- *Read.* Read to him and with him. Let him see you and his dad reading. Make regular trips to the public library, and let him get his own library card as soon as he's old enough. Buy books for him from time to time. Let him keep his own collection of special books.

- *Investigate.* Expose him to nature, and questions will inevitably surface. If you don't know the answers, make a game of finding them. Find answers to his questions in books and, sometimes, on the Internet. Let him know that his questions and their answers are important.
- *Inquire.* When he asks a question, ask him, "What do you think?" Give him the opportunity to think aloud and work through his ideas verbally.
- *Observe.* Realize that your boys may have different learning styles. (You'll find more about this in chapter 4, "The Education of Boys.") Remember that different boys express their curiosity in different ways. Observe different signals from different sons.
- *Learn.* Show that you value learning. At the dinner table, in the car, wherever you can, talk about what you've seen and done and read. As a family, discuss lessons learned from a movie or television program. Watch informational, documentary programs together and discuss them.

Look for and utilize each teachable moment. Sometimes you can just see curiosity on a boy's face—there's a question in his mind if not on his lips. Don't ignore it! Take advantage of the teachable moment to encourage his natural curiosity and develop his love of learning.

Cultivate Them Socially

Boys need to learn to interact socially with others, and they need your help to learn how. If you're the mother of multiple boys, you have a built-in social group, and sibling interaction can help your boys learn social skills. Even more, it's important that boys understand how to act in different social situations. You can't expect him to just pick it up on his own. Some boys will, but an intentional mom understands that her sons are different from each other and is aware of each son's needs. Before you arrive at a party or a friend's house or a restaurant, remind the boys about acceptable behavior. By the time my sons were born, I'd seen a number of kids that weren't enjoyable to be around. The last thing I wanted was for people to roll their eyes and shake their heads as they thought of my boys. Instead, I wanted people to enjoy being around my sons. I spent a lot of time saying, "We don't do this" and "We *do* do this." I don't think boys should deny who they really are and become total pleasers, but they do need to understand the boundaries of acceptable social interaction.

One of the easiest ways to train boys how to act in public is to train them to act in an acceptable manner at home. If they say "Please" and "Thank you" at home, they're more likely to say it in a social setting. The best way to ingrain such habits is by modeling. My sons know what their jobs are around the house, but I still thank them for doing their chores. When they carry in the groceries, I tell them thank you. When they help me on the computer, I tell them thank you. When their dad takes us out to dinner or a movie, I remind the boys to thank him for taking us out for a fun evening.

Common courtesy begins at home, and if you begin teaching it when your boys are young, it will surface at the appropriate times later. Even when your sons are small, take time to include them in writing thank-you notes for gifts. Just because they're boys doesn't mean they can't show appreciation. Instead of the traditional thank-you note, let them color or draw a truck or use the computer to create a card—just help your boys make the effort to show gratitude. (For more on boys, manners, and social situations, see chapter 8, "Growing Respect.")

As your boys begin to socialize with peers, make time for their friends. Let them take turns asking a friend over to the house or along on an excursion. It can be tiring, I know—I often felt like saying no to having their friends over. I had enough boys in the house without adding another. But it's important to the social development of each one of your sons. Proverbs 27:17 reminds us, "As iron sharpens iron, so one man sharpens another." Our desire is for our sons to be honed in a godly direction, so we must encourage them to form good relationships.

It's important, as well, to know the parents of your sons' friends. Those parents can, in fact, become your allies. Your son may tell you that you're the only parent who has a certain rule, but that's not always the case. When our first son got his driver's license, he was not allowed to drive with friends in the car for a period of time. He and three other boys met for an accountability group and then went to a local restaurant. When he got home, I asked if they left some of the cars somewhere when they went to eat. He sighed and said, "No, Mom... everybody's parents have the same rule, so none of us could drive each other. We took a caravan of four minivans to the restaurant." That was rather affirming!

Taking advantage of organized activities definitely adds to your boys' social skills. Church and neighborhood activities and organized sports all play a part in adding to your sons' socialization. Our sons all played T-ball and baseball. (Four games on a Saturday made for a long day!) That worked for a while, but as the boys grew they acquired different preferences and skills. We experimented, trying to get them all to like the same things, but realized that after initially forming a foundation for them and introducing them all to what we felt was valuable, we then needed to watch for individual interest. We then tried to allow each to express his own preference in extracurricular activities. There was some diversity to their preferences, and we did a bit of juggling at times, trying not to overcommit, but we strove to give each boy some opportunity to pursue what he loved best.

In the area of social skills, dialogue is important, too. Keep your eyes and ears open and talk about the good and bad that you observe. Lessons may come from a scenario you witness in the grocery store, waiting for the school bus, or in a movie or television program. Point out the positives and negatives of the social situations you see. As my boys have grown, I've tried to point out examples of both wise and unwise choices. "What do you think would have happened if he had …" has become a valuable question in our dialogue.

Some social situations are difficult for boys, but it's important to use those as learning experiences. I remember the day my eldest son jumped into the car at school and blurted out, "I just want you to homeschool me!" He'd hit upon rocky times with friends at school, and he just wanted out. We talked about it and used the situation to teach him coping skills. He came through it unscathed (and in chapter 10, "A Word from the Boys," he makes an interesting observation about the lessons of that time).

Social skills are first learned at home, so the tone you set there will make a difference in how your sons approach their daily situations. In *Bringing Up Boys*, Dobson writes about a relational concept called "the first five minutes." Researchers have documented that the first five minutes of any encounter will set the tone for all that is to follow. The first five minutes of the morning will set the tone for the ride to school, and perhaps your son's attitude toward the day. The first five minutes after school can color family relationships for the rest of the evening and beyond.[4] If Mom is aware, careful, and prayerful about the first five minutes, it can make a big difference in how interactions go throughout the day. Teaching your sons the same as they grow will help them as they approach social situations.

Nourish Them Spiritually

The importance of our sons' spiritual nurturing is perhaps best expressed in *Parenting Isn't for Cowards* by James Dobson: "I urge you as parents of young children, whether compliant or strong-willed, to provide for them an unshakable faith in Jesus Christ. This is your most important function as mothers and fathers. How can anything else compare in significance to the goal of keeping the family circle unbroken in the life to come? What an incredible objective to work toward."[5]

And as we look at life here and now, it's easy to see that nurturing our sons spiritually lays a foundation for so much. Meg Meeker cites research that shows the benefits of a spiritual life for boys. She writes that research has consistently shown that religion

- helps kids stay away from drugs.
- helps keep kids away from sexual activity.
- helps keep kids away from smoking.
- gives kids moral guidance.
- gives them significantly higher self-esteem and more positive attitudes.
- contributes to their growing maturity as they pass from childhood through adolescence.
- helps them set boundaries and stay out of trouble.
- helps teens keep a good perspective on life.
- helps teens feel good and be happy.
- helps teens experience fewer depressive symptoms.
- helps most teens get through their problems and troubles.
- helps kids feel better about their bodies and physical appearance.
- helps increase "learned competence" in leadership skills, coping skills, and cultural capital.[6]

As Christian parents, we know firsthand the benefits of a strong spiritual life. As mothers of boys, we face days we couldn't get through without a loving, sovereign God to lean on. But remember, we've had years to reach the spiritual plains on which we now stand, and we are adults. Two words are extremely important when it comes to your sons and their faith: *individuality* and *balance*. Each boy is unique and will respond in his own way, in God's time, to spiritual lessons. We can't expect each son to respond the same when it comes to spiritual matters. We must allow them the freedom to listen and learn and weigh and make their faith their own.

Individuality goes hand-in-hand with balance. A mother's attitude toward spiritual matters must not be relentless or harsh. No matter how hard we push or what memorization we require, spiritual decisions are heart matters, ultimately between each boy and God. We must teach and live the truth of Scripture and show our Savior's love, but we cannot legislate our boys' hearts. For our sons to see the difference between God's way and the world's way, our homes must be different from the world.

In her book, *Your Boy*, Vicki Courtney outlines the world's equations for defining one's self-worth. She says boys are susceptible to these three equations:

> Worth = What You Look Like
> Worth = What You Do
> Worth = What Other People Think[7]

If our homes are places where our sons are valued for who they are in Christ, our boys will see the difference between what the world defines as worth and what God defines as worth. If we can be "joyful in hope, patient in affliction, faithful in prayer" (Rom. 12:12), our sons will see our faith daily. Here are more ways to emphasize spiritual values in your home:

- *Modeling.* It's crucial that a mom look to her own heart. It's hard to scream at the boys when strains of a praise song are playing in the background, so use music to strengthen your walk and witness.
- *Singing.* Sing to (and with) your sons at bedtime—hymns, Sunday school songs, popular Christian music. Sing to them from the time they're babes in arms.
- *Bible reading.* Age-appropriate Bible story books have short stories perfect for reading right before bedtime. Introduce

your boys to strong male models in the men of the Bible, using the traits of biblical figures to show your boys how to live. There are plenty of good Christian resources—books and DVDs—that can help as we strive to raise our boys to love Christ and show His love to others.

- *Having family devotions.* If you have school-age to teen sons, consider Tim Shoemaker's *Dangerous Devotions for Guys.*[8] It's full of active, visual devotionals with real lessons—a great family resource.

A Praying Mom

Prayer is vital in the Christian life, and its place in the Christian family should be paramount. Philippians 4:6 reminds us: "Do not be anxious about anything, but in everything, by prayer and petition, with thanksgiving, present your requests to God." Praying before each meal together seems like a small ritual when your boys are little, but it makes a big impact when it's carried on when they're teens and have friends over, or the family is eating in a restaurant. Bedtime prayer after songs and stories has been a given for our boys, and I think it's served them well.

In times of uncertainty or upheaval, make prayer the family's first reaction. We prayed with the boys as we prepared for Hurricane Andrew here in Florida; we prayed when we heard of the death of a beloved teacher; we prayed on 9/11; we prayed before pulling out of the driveway each time we set out for vacation. Those times serve as memory markers for the boys. In times of grief, uncertainty, or anticipation, the family turned toward God.

Mom, let's not forget the daily prayers we lift up—the short, murmured, "Lord, bring them home safely" or "Lord, get him up off that football field." If I awake in the night, I figure it must be for a reason, and I use the time to pray for my family. A time that could be distressing turns into a time of blessing.

The best thing an intentional mom can do for her sons is to pray. If they aren't following your timetable on spiritual matters, don't give up. Remember that they express themselves in different ways; be patient. Know that they're in the Lord's hands; He knows them well. Psalm 139:16 assures us that all their days were written in God's book before one of your sons ever came to be. The best thing you can do for them is to intercede on their behalf.

Let your sons know that you love the Lord, and that you love them. Communicate to your boys by your words and actions that they are of worth—uniquely, individually loved by our Creator. We are reminded in Luke 12:7, "Indeed, the very hairs of your head are all numbered. Don't be afraid; you are worth more than many sparrows." When we learn to love our sons as He does, intentional parenting becomes easier, and it reaps great rewards in loving mother-son relationships.

4

The Education of Boys

For wisdom will enter your heart,
and knowledge will be pleasant to your soul.
PROVERBS 2:10

That wisdom will enter their hearts and knowledge will be pleasant to their souls is certainly our hope for our boys. The problem is, knowledge is anything but pleasant to some boys because of their aversion to school. This isn't true of all boys, of course, but as you'll see in this chapter, even experts contend that many of our schools are set up to the detriment of boys. Our job is to prepare them to survive—and thrive—in that atmosphere. There's much we as moms can do to support our boys' school life: we can help form positive attitudes toward learning, maintain a good study atmosphere at home, and establish good communication between parent and teacher. But before all of that—and during it, too—it's important to consider your son's balance of school and play.

Play Is a Child's First Job

My perspective on boys and play is a unique one, having been both a mom of four boys and a middle school and high school English teacher. I took the education classes that talked about developmental stages, and then I got to see the need for play firsthand in my own sons. In addition, my own high school classroom has yielded valuable information about how boys act and interact in an educational setting. Having seen both ends of the spectrum, I agree with the experts who tell us that the biological, developmental, and social differences between males and females often make the school setting a difficult one for boys.

Young boys are less mature, less verbal, and more active than girls of their age. Girls may be able to sit quietly with a crayon, while boys need safe outlets for their activity. A wise preschool teacher once told me, "Play is a child's first job." The authors of *Einstein Never Used Flash Cards*, two mothers with their doctorates in education and psychology, put it this way: "Play is to early childhood what gas is to a car... it is the very fuel of every intellectual activity that our children engage in."[1] What goes on in a child's play is vital to later learning. In a society where information will be increasingly at our fingertips, the need will increase, too, for people who can process and apply information in a creative way. Creative problem solvers, not memorizers, will have valuable skills, and creative problem solving has its roots in play.

If we are to foster learning in our sons, we must realize that boys are hands on. Most of them learn through activity—they're kinesthetic learners. A boy needs to be able to explore cause and effect, to daydream, to create castles in his own mind. And he needs balance in his play—some should be with Mom and/or Dad (or a trusted adult male), some with siblings and friends, and some play should take place alone. So don't discount the importance of play in your son's life—no matter what his age.

It's a Boy's Life for Me!

If you have a toddler, provide creative toys for him that he can manipulate. Stay away from any kind of screen! There's plenty of time for television and computers when he's older. Perhaps choose an occasional educational program to watch (check out the suggestions in chapter 7). An endless stream of DVDs may seem convenient for you, but look at your toddler—he takes on a zombie-like appearance when he's watching. If he becomes conditioned to being entertained electronically, when he gets older you'll be competing with those DVDs for a snippet of conversation.

If you have an elementary-age son, don't assume his play days are behind him. Many parents insist that their children sit down and do homework as soon as they get home from school.

My boys always had a quick snack and some downtime before we hit the books. Boys need to burn off some energy before sitting down to do what they've done all day. Their bodies and their minds need to release some steam. On some afternoons I insisted the boys go outside for twenty minutes; they were bouncing off the walls inside the house! Usually that twenty minutes passed all too quickly and I found myself calling them in an hour later.

If you have a teenage son, he may be involved in sports that hold after-school practices and he can burn off plenty of steam. Teenagers involved in sports come home hungry and often beat. I still find they need a little conversation and a few minutes of downtime before tackling homework. Just set limits—"Take about thirty minutes after dinner to do what you want before starting your homework." If your son isn't involved in any sports, be sure he remains active. Encourage him to run, walk, or bike. We all need more exercise than we get, so maybe you can turn a walk into family time. You can walk and talk.

Creative Play

Encourage active play among your boys, and avoid using weekends and summers to vegetate in front of the television. Remember the sticks, string, and boxes from chapter 1? Keep an ample supply of those. Encourage creative play. Until they were middle-school age, my boys dressed up as Indians, cowboys, detectives... daily, it seemed. They had great games and even shot a few videos—those are priceless now. Set aside a special box or bin for costumes—hats, holsters, vests, masks. Foster creativity and imagination in your boys. Doubtless their games will be different from those you played as a child, but they'll have a great time pretending to save the world, the kingdom, or maybe even Mom.

Reading is a great launching place for adventure (as detailed in chapter 7). Stories provide all kinds of inspiration for creative play. I highly recommend *The Dangerous Book for Boys* by brothers

Conn and Hal Iggulden. The foreword states, "In this age of video games and cell phones, there must still be a place for knots, tree houses, and stories of incredible courage."[2] This book contains extraordinary stories, and covers everything from the greatest paper airplane in the world to timers and tripwires to understanding grammar and making cloth fireproof.

Some of boys' best adventures take place outside, so get those boys out of the house. As our society becomes more tied to computer and media, we lose sight of the wonder of God's creation. Today's culture makes it increasingly easy to overlook the benefits of nature, but research tells us that exposure to nature is crucial. Richard Louv writes in *Last Child in the Woods*, "A growing body of evidence indicates that direct exposure to nature is essential for physical and emotional health. For example, new studies suggest that exposure to nature may reduce the symptoms of Attention Deficit Hyperactivity Disorder, and that it can improve all children's cognitive abilities and resistance to negative stresses and depression."[3] Nature lends itself to creative play, gives boys an opportunity to run off some of that energy, and reminds us of our Creator—so get those boys outside!

And last, Mom—be fun! Yes, boys need safety and security and structure, but they also need downtime with you. You'll help make memories if you contribute to their play, serve as audience, or even wholeheartedly participate. You won't lose their respect or your place of authority. They'll respect you even more if you're able to appreciate all aspects of their boyhood. Of course you love them when they obey and comply, but love them when they clown and climb, and they'll really know that you love them.

Boys and School

Keeping an aspect of play in our boys' lives is important especially as they enter the school arena. So much about school, however, is not oriented to boys. The elementary classroom is largely language-based and, on average, girls are stronger than boys in language. The average boy is not as mature as the average girl at school age, and the person standing in front of the elementary classroom is much more likely to be a woman than a man. My boys have had some wonderful women teachers—most that I would place in that category have had sons of their own. That's certainly not a requirement for being a good elementary teacher, but some firsthand exposure to boys at home can certainly help a teacher understand the male animal.

If girls are socially and developmentally ahead of boys in preschool or kindergarten, you can see the problem. Who is the teacher to hold those girls back? Therefore, the atmosphere is often geared more toward the quiet reader who has outstanding fine motor skills—and that's not the boy. Further, school has changed. Years ago, children were not expected to learn to read in kindergarten; now they are. School has changed, but the nature of boys remains the same.

Researchers tell us that boys learn differently from girls because of their biological composition. In *The Wonder of Girls*, Michael Gurian explains how higher blood flow in the female brain creates a higher ability to maintain attention on others: "The female brain is, by genetic structure, less prone to an attention problem because it is internally, inherently and more consistently attending to her and to the flow of connections, lessons, learning and relationships."[4] Yes, there are boys who excel in the classroom. The difficulty lies in the fact that they have to overcome biological and natural predispositions to do so. Statistics tell the story when boys don't overcome those predispositions:

- Boys receive lower grades and are more likely to repeat a grade than are girls.
- Boys perform significantly below girls in reading and writing.
- Boys have a higher high-school dropout rate than girls.

- Parents of boys are contacted twice as often as parents of girls about their child's behavior or schoolwork.
- Boys' suspensions from school represent almost three-fourths of all school suspensions.
- Two-thirds of all special education students are boys.[5]

These statistics paint a pretty bleak picture, don't they? Whether or not your son falls into those above categories, many boys do, and that affects the environment that your son is called to survive in.

If your son does well in school, he'll likely have a number of friends who do not. The attitudes of the less successful boys toward school and their peers will be affected by their lack of success, and your son will need to deal with those peers. It's often not easy for a boy to excel in school because of pressure from other boys who view success in a different light. That's why the ultimate answer to this dilemma for you and your sons lies in their perception of who they are and what they're worth. But before we get to that, let's discuss specific ways you can help your sons survive school.

Developing School Survival Skills

You'll get a head start on developing school survival skills if you foster curiosity and learning early. I've always felt my goal was to teach my boys to love learning, for that's a lifelong asset. A love of learning will serve them well after the high school and college years. Technology changes at such a rapid pace today that tomorrow's worker will be called upon to continue learning long after the first day on the job. A love of learning enhances one's personal life as well. Reading newspapers and magazines, for instance—either the old-fashioned way or via the Internet—gives us a view of the world and others. Studying Scripture reveals more about ourselves and our Creator. Your adult son will enjoy acquiring information about new places and things, about himself and about God if you work to instill in him a life-time love of learning. How can you do that?

- Let your boys play, and play with them.
- Read to them and let them read to you.
- Talk at mealtimes and at other times about what you see, read, and experience.
- Watch the news together when they're old enough, then discuss what you've seen.
- Let them see you and your husband read. Make the newspaper available to them and encourage them to read what they can. Many papers have sections for children, complete with activities.
- Take educational trips—across town or across the country. Visit historical sites to help your boys develop a sense of history.

These kinds of activities not only lay the groundwork for a lifetime love of learning, they help keep you involved with your sons.

Handling Rough Spots in the Classroom

No matter how much your boys enjoy the educational activities you provide at home, they may still hit some rough spots in the classroom. You can help them over the bumpy stretches by establishing good communication with your son's teacher.

First, in non-threatening language, let his teacher know how your son learns best. For example, "We use Scrabble tiles at home to spell out the spelling words, and that seems to help him." Every bit of information you can give will help the teacher know him better.

Second, tell her about his hobbies and abilities. Share his positive comments about school with her. We teachers love to hear what is working. We need to know what impact our teaching is having on students.

Third, if you have to share some bad news, do it carefully, without threatening the teacher's authority. As a teacher, I can tell you that it hurts to hear a mom say, "My son doesn't think you like him." Maybe the boy's perception is wrong, but no one can deny he feels that way. I've found that some boys just need a few more strokes than others—more positive verbal feedback in the classroom. As a teacher, I'm not necessarily communicating I don't like a student; instead, I'm just not communicating that I do. If you let a teacher know what works for your son—what has been successful for you—that will give him or her a better understanding of how to reach your son.

If you're able to help your son over educational road bumps while showing respect for the student, the teacher, and the classroom, you'll communicate even bigger life lessons to him.

Talking About School Difficulties

If your dialogue with your son's teacher is less than positive, be careful about how much you share with your son. If you're not satisfied and feel you need to talk to an administrator, do so; but if your son is feeling bitter toward his teacher, don't fuel that. You need to show support and respect for his teachers if you expect him to do the same. As we deal with this issue, 1 Thessalonians 5:12 is instructive for us and our sons: "Now we ask you, brothers, to respect those who work hard among you, who are over you in the Lord and who admonish you." Our modeling of respect speaks volumes to our sons.

Let your sons know that, while they can talk to you about school difficulties, some things are best not shared with brothers. My boys attended a unit school that went from preschool to grade twelve. That meant several of my sons had the same teacher at one point or another in their schooling. Negative talk around the dinner table about the fifth-grade teacher was not a good idea. More than once, I pulled a son aside and said, "I understand you're not crazy about how Mr. Brown teaches history, but you can't prejudice your little brother about that. Watch what you say in front of him." They had to learn that what they said affected their little brothers' perception of teachers and often school in general. If your son encounters some difficulty in school, let him know he can come to you. Brothers can help, and are often good sounding boards, but your son needs to know you care about his school day.

Taking Positive Steps

Prepare your son for the classroom by placing him in situations where similar behavior is required. Sunday school is a great first classroom. We don't all talk at once, there's a story time, and you have to wait your turn. Establishing limits for your sons and holding them to those limits will prepare them for the rules encountered in the classroom. Taking your son to age-appropriate concerts and plays while he's still a preschooler will teach him about situations that are for sitting still and watching and listening—valuable abilities in the classroom.

At home, establish and maintain a good study atmosphere. After the boys have let off some steam at the end of a school day, have a quiet place for them to study or do homework. A quiet place is free from the distractions of the television or computer. At that time, in that place, schoolwork rules. If they do their homework in the family room and one son finishes his homework early, he needs to find something to occupy himself in another room. The TV in the family room should remain off until all studying is done.

And Mom needs to be available to help. Offer to review with your son before a test—all the way to high school. I've learned it's better to *assume* than to *ask*. "Here, let me quiz you on that" often elicits a reluctant "Okay" while "Do you want some help studying?" would likely be answered, "No, I'm okay."

Encourage your boys to help each other as well. They need to learn the value of spurring "one another on toward love and good deeds" (Heb. 10:24), and they can help one another. But do remember that what worked for one son may not work for the next. One of my boys recopied his spelling words three times to get ready for a spelling test, while his auditory brother used a tape recorder to record the word and its spelling. He listened to the tape and wrote the words down as he heard them. Different strokes for different boys. Since boys are more activity-oriented, some like to do some kinesthetic activity to help them review, like writing on a blackboard or drawing letters in the air as they spell the word aloud. Find out what works best for your son and encourage him to use that as he studies.

The boys-plus household has an advantage, as sisters provide more opportunities for boys to see how girls approach reading and writing. Seeing a sister enjoy those activities may pique a boy's desire for the same. Be careful, though, about stereotyping and labeling. If your daughter truly does enjoy reading, it's fine to acknowledge that. It's not healthy, though, to use her particular preference to shame a boy—or worse, to limit his potential by expecting him to react "as boys do." Remember, your children's worth lies in who they are to God, not in what they can and can't do in the classroom. None of your daughter's abilities or your son's skills makes them more—or less—valuable to the One who made them.

Loving Unconditionally

Perhaps the best advice in helping your boys survive and thrive in the school atmosphere came from a mother I know well. When one of my sons was not achieving the way I thought he should and could, I poured out all my concerns to her. At the time, I thought her advice was simplistic and vague, but I've since found it to be so true. She said to me, "Honey, just love him."

I immediately thought, "Of course, I love him!" It took some time for me to realize what she was saying: despite everything—even with lack of achievement, bad attitudes, disinterest in something I thought was so important—I needed to let him know that I loved him. The apostle Paul's beautiful lesson on love in 1 Corinthians 13 teaches us that our love truly must be unconditional. We can teach our boys about faith, we can instill hope in them, and we can love them, but "the greatest of these is love" (v. 13). And that love can't be tied to achievement in school or sports or music, or to hairstyle. In spite of our sons' flaws and foibles, we need to love them. Somehow you must learn to communicate to your boy that you will love him no more or less—homerun or foul out, A or D, clean-cut hair or fringe that goes to his nose.

Truly loving unconditionally is hard because it entails giving up our own expectations (remember chapter 1?). We need to remind ourselves of the blessing we've been given; we need to understand that God made our boys the way they are for a reason; we need to ask for wisdom in dealing with the way they are. It's easy to fall into that expectation pit when you have several children of the same sex. Yes, they're somewhat alike, but we must remember that, not only will boys be boys, but boys will be different boys.

Ask the Lord to let you in on who your son really is. Each one of your boys is "fearfully and wonderfully made" (Ps. 139:14). Look for what he really loves and what makes him light up. What kind of praise does he respond to best? What does he show a bent toward—be it academic or mechanical or musical? Find out and use that to help him in his learning. Reinforce his strengths and show him how to use them to his best advantage. Accept that he may not be what you have in mind for him to be. Most of all, trust him to the Lord and ask Him to guide you and your son.

Education in Perspective

As a high school teacher, I love my subject area and I value academics. But I often tell parents that what serves their kids in the long run are things we don't always reward in the educational setting: determination, persistence, dependability, a strong work ethic—not to mention godly character. You and your son will be strengthened through tough times at school if you remember, "We also rejoice in our sufferings, because we know that suffering produces perseverance; perseverance, character; and character, hope" (Rom. 5:3–4). If you can capitalize on your son's stubbornness and turn it into persistence in school, you'll be doing him a great favor. A dependable student who turns in everything and gives it his best may not be the straight-A student, but in life, he'll be a success at what he undertakes.

I've met parents who were hoping for remarkable students. Instead, their kids are only average students with remarkable personalities. Those students, though, will prevail in the right situation. They are people-oriented, and if their self-esteem remains intact, they'll be able to use that remarkable personality to achieve what God has for them in life. And determination, dependability, and strong work ethic? Most employers today would describe the model employee using exactly those characteristics. A son who displays them is doing the best with what God has given to him, whether or not his report card has an "A" on it.

If you can acknowledge your son's weaknesses as well as his strengths, there's a greater chance you'll let him learn from failure. As moms, we're tempted to try to protect our sons from ever failing, but it's important to remember that failure can be a great teacher. Thomas Edison experimented more than a hundred times before he invented the working light bulb, and he later stated that he learned something from each failure that eventually led to his success. Boys learn resilience when we moms neither exaggerate their mistakes nor rescue them from failure. If we talk with them about the nature of the failure and why it happened, and guide them to what can be learned from it, we'll be nurturing their self-esteem.[6]

Protecting your son's self-esteem is crucial. If your son has the confidence that he is loved by God and loved by you regardless of his achievements, he'll be equipped to face giants. All children reach an age when peer acceptance becomes important, but if your son is well-grounded in who he is and how valuable he is, he'll be less susceptible to the changing winds of what and who his peers accept. If you begin early to instill in your son that he is valuable to God and you, that he is special and unique, and that he can go wherever and do whatever God leads, he'll be well-prepared for those turbulent middle and high school years when peers seem to gain importance.

Your son may not be Ivy League (or Major League) material, and if you expected otherwise, you need to let go of those expectations. Dr. Meg Meeker writes, "Having done all you can do to help, accept the best he can give. Go with the flow and begin searching for other areas of success."[7] Find his loves and his talents and capitalize on those, always reinforcing the importance of a work ethic. We do our best in all things as if for the Lord, whether or not we're the best at it. "Whatever you do, work at it with all your heart, as working for the Lord, not for men, since you know that you will receive an inheritance from the Lord as a reward. It is the Lord Christ you are serving" (Col. 3:23–24).

I tell my students the story of a little boy who gave a necklace to his mom. It was a gift and she said, "Thank you," but she thought it was small and insignificant, and she never wore it. The little boy watched and watched, but he never saw his gift being used by his mom. All of our abilities, be they large or small, are gifts from God. Consider how that little boy felt, and perhaps you can see how it must grieve our Creator when we disregard the gifts He has given us, simply because we feel they're not the best.

Chances are, ten years after your son leaves school, his grades for handwriting in elementary school won't matter. But he'll probably remember how you reacted to it. "We just want you to do your best" became our mantra when our boys were in school. Realizing that each one was different was one of the hardest things for me to accept as a mom. As a teacher, I would have loved for my sons to be four scholars. But my prayer is ultimately to have four godly young men who work as if for the Lord in all they do, as they share His love with those around them.

5

Boy Talk

He who answers before listening—that is his folly
and his shame.

PROVERBS 18:13

One of a boy mom's greatest tasks is to encourage her sons to listen to others and to express themselves. We know that women and men communicate differently, and our goal as moms should be to help our sons bridge that gap. If we can help make our sons comfortable with conversation, and if we model effective communication for them, they'll grow up with an understanding of male/female differences in communication styles, and they'll have a better idea of how to cope with them. If we don't provide that understanding, our sons will grow up truly believing that "men are from Mars, women are from Venus" and they'll be ill-equipped for relationships.

As a boy mom, you are the standard for your sons when it comes to female communication. You are the constant in their lives, and they often have few other female examples on which to base their attitudes and decisions. Teaching and modeling effective methods of communication will not only benefit our sons in the future, it will strengthen the mother-son relationship. Here are some advantages to establishing strong communication:

- With strong mother-son lines of communication, the odds of having a silent, sullen teenage son decrease.
- Nurturing brother-to-brother communication will lay the foundation for strong family ties in years to come.
- A young man who knows how to listen and express himself has a strong foundation for his own family and relationships. If you can teach your sons to talk, your future daughters-in-law will thank you!

Early Talk

A boy mom often begins with a set of preconceived notions about communicating with her son—he won't talk, he doesn't talk, he doesn't like to talk. These can very well be true, but too often moms *make* them true—they become self-fulfilling prophecies. Many boy moms don't take the time to talk with their young sons because they assume boys can't, don't, or won't converse. If we begin with that preconceived mind-set, we give up on fostering our sons' communication skills.

The first thing a boy mom must do is leave those expectations behind and talk to her son. In *The Everything Parent's Guide to Raising Boys,* Erwin writes of a revealing study that found that mothers encouraged language skills equally in sons and daughters until babies reached about eight months. Boy babies, however, generally become more physically active at that age, and mothers began to emphasize language less and let their sons focus more on physical development than on language.[1] Don't make that mistake. From the beginning, deluge your sons with language. Narrate everyday life for your young son, even before he can speak. He's adding up all those experiences in a little bank that he'll draw from one day. So even while he's still cooing in his baby seat, tell him about your plans for the day, what the weather looks like, and how the traffic light goes from green to yellow to red.

When our first son was about a year old, we drove past a fire station. Dad not only pointed it out, he began telling Jonathan what happens when the fire bell rings. "The bell will ring, and the firemen will roll out of their beds and get their coats and hats on. They slide down the pole and jump on to the truck and the big door goes up ... " At the time, I smiled to myself and thought, *Jonathan is not getting a word of this.* But my husband continued to take that approach whenever he was with the boys. To this day, when they see a truck or a device or a piece of equipment, they ask their dad how it works or what it does. I did my part at home, narrating the making of peanut butter sandwiches and the sorting of laundry. I firmly believe that immersion in language provided our boys with

- a familiarity with communication skills.
- a base of knowledge about everyday things.
- a natural curiosity about things and how they work.

Moms aren't limited, however, to narration and technical talk. When you read or watch something together, don't hesitate to ask your son, "How does Pooh look here? Is he happy or sad?" Kindlon and Thompson in *Raising Cain* write about research into communicating emotions. The study shows that mothers speak about emotions, like sadness and distress, with their daughters more than with their sons. Even fathers and older siblings speak to younger boys more about information than about feelings.[2] Instead of avoiding talk about emotions, recognize that early talk that identifies emotions can make later talk about such things easier. And if your son does initiate conversations abut his feelings, resist the temptation to finish his sentences or jump ahead and provide a response he hasn't yet asked for. Take a deep breath, be patient, and let him put his thoughts together in words.

Some young children seem to be naturally hesitant about communicating. If your son is like this, remind him to "use his words." Don't let him gesture for everything, but wait for the spoken word. Here are a few more hints for helping the reluctant talker:

- Get on the floor with your child or at his eye level as you talk with him.
- Ask questions and give him time to respond.
- Provide a play telephone or play microphone to encourage his chatter.

And don't forget to write down the priceless things you hear him say.

School Talk

Once your sons enter school, be ready and interested to hear about their day. Ask leading questions that will promote conversation. "How was your day today?" will probably only elicit a "Good" from your son. But if you ask, "What happened on the playground today?" or "Who did you sit with at lunch?" you'll be more likely to stimulate conversation.

As your sons learn to express themselves, reinforce manners in conversation. After-school talk and dinnertime conversation are great times to do this. Remind your sons to wait until another is done talking and not to chime in and "steal their brother's thunder" when that brother is telling a story or joke. Teach them to be considerate listeners as well as good conversationalists.

Those skills will help your sons in a variety of ways. For example, listening skills can help school-age boys solve conflict. In the midst of a dispute, children often lash out without really listening to one another. Be ready to step into sibling conflicts and say, "Wait a minute. John, did you hear what Nate said?" James 1:19 reminds us, "Everyone should be quick to listen, slow to speak and slow to become angry." Teach your boys to listen and to talk through whatever problems they can.

Moms need to realize, too, that the talk—the stories—they get at home about events at school can be exaggerated or misunderstood. When your son accuses someone of something or confesses to his own wrongdoing, it's always best to get another perspective to go along with his school-age viewpoint. Call his teacher and see if she or he is aware of what went on. A teacher can often lend another perspective to the situation that your son isn't attuned to, and that can help you deal with the situation.

When your son comes home and reports a schoolyard conflict, ask him to remember as clearly as possible who said what. Then ask him, "Why do you think Billy said that? What would have been a better thing to say?" Teach him balance as you explore the day's events. Don't dismiss his stories as unimportant, but don't forget to end with something like, "What was the best thing that happened today?" or "What was the most fun thing you did?"

All of us have dealt with school-age children who exaggerate or boast. If your son has a friend who does this, it's best to handle your reaction carefully. If your son tells you, "Jake said his dad is going to buy him a horse!" a maternal outburst like, "Oh, that's not true!" will immediately set your son on the defensive. He doesn't want to believe that anything his friend says might not be true. You may, in fact, end up on the opposite side of your son as he exclaims, "You just don't like my friends!" A measured, rational approach will work better with him. Prefacing your comments with an unemotional, "Now, think about this" will help. Then you can follow up with, "Do Jake's parents have room for a horse in their garage?" Guide them to value truth. When the time is right, remind your sons of Proverbs 14:25: "A truthful witness saves lives, but a false witness is deceitful."

Teen Talk

Most kids generally get less communicative as they enter their teen years. Establishing a strong foundation early for mother-son communication will help preclude to some extent the grunt and nod responses. But some of it just comes with the territory. In *Bringing Up Boys*, Dobson warns that boys may be "concealing a cauldron of emotion," and he advises, "When you see a closed spirit developing, don't let another day go by without bringing hidden feelings out in the open. It's the first principle of healthy family life."[3]

How can you help your teen to talk? Here are a few suggestions:

- Understand his communication style. One of my sons will tell me almost anything, but another plays everything close to the vest. One likes to talk in the car and another opens up across the table if you have him alone in a restaurant. At times you have to play those cards to get them talking. If you're intentional enough to let your son know that you understand his communication style, that will go a long way toward strengthening the mother-son bond.

- Let him talk. Don't stop him mid-sentence to ask for detail or clarification. Wait! If you stop him, you may not get him talking again.
- Don't expect him to communicate like you do. You want more, of course—women thrive on description and detail, but you won't get it by saying, "Tell me more." You'll need to ask specific questions when he seems finished, like "What did she say after you turned your homework in?" or "What kind of car was he driving?"
- Don't be afraid to ask, "How did that make you feel?" but realize that you may get a blank stare. If you ask, "What did you think about that?" you'll probably get a more insightful answer.
- Provide opportunities to talk. Make it a priority for the family to have dinner together, even if it has to be late, after football practice, or after Dad gets home. The inconvenience or disruption of your schedule will pay off in a closer family bond. Leave the television and music off—make it a time that's conducive to conversation.

Table Talk

Dinnertime conversation is just one practice that, if begun early, will be more likely to continue as your sons grow. In today's who-has-time society, there's more need than ever for the shared family meal. Meal times are about more than just eating. Our boys can learn, share, and participate in civilized society at the dinner table. (There's more about that civilized society in chapter 8, "Growing Respect.") A family that eats together regularly and provides a safe haven for their children to speak and listen and explore is immunizing them against an often hostile culture. In *Bringing Up Boys*, Dobson cites several studies that support the value of family meals. Studies reveal that adolescents who ate dinner with parents at least five times per week were least likely to

- be on drugs.
- be depressed.
- be in trouble with the law.

They were more likely to

- be doing well in school.
- be surrounded by a circle of supportive friends.

It's of note that the same benefits were found whether the families ate in restaurants or at home; breaking bread together was the key factor.[4]

The importance of family meals for teens should not be underestimated. In *The Surprising Power of Family Meals*, Miriam Weinstein cites studies by CASA (The National Center on Addiction and Substance Abuse) as she writes about a troubling disconnect: "Just at the time when substance abuse rises, from ages twelve to seventeen, is the time when family dinners decline."[5] Only one-third of high school juniors and seniors have dinner with their families on a regular basis. Weinstein warns, "It's easy to lose track of the fact that they still need the regular contact, the feeling that they are part of a group. They still need and crave adult guidance, even if they communicate the opposite."[6]

Family mealtimes are a perfect opportunity to provide that guidance. As Christian families discuss what happened that day, they're exploring the practicality of God's truth. Such discussions have long-lasting effects. Proverbs 4:20–22 reminds us: "My son, pay attention to what I say; listen closely to my words. Do not let them out of your sight, keep them within your heart;

for they are life to those who find them and health to a man's whole body." Family mealtimes can lead to conversation and interaction about what's really important in life, and those lessons stay within sight and stick close to the heart.

It's easier to maintain family mealtimes with teens if the habit is established early. Family mealtimes with your toddler can begin a tradition that will last well into the teen years. If, though, your children are already well into school or teen years, it's not too late to start.

- If you can't do dinner together every night right now, at least start somewhere. First, choose two nights a week, then gradually transition toward more regular family meal times.
- Family meals should be positive, meaningful events, not opportunities to criticize. Be as positive as possible when at the table, and teach your boys that some things are better addressed at a different time and place.
- Involve your sons in the conversation. You and Dad may have to wait until later to carry on your conversation, but make sure mealtime conversation includes everyone.

Don't fall for, "He's a teen, so the last thing he'll want to do is eat with us." That's what society tells us, but a teen, more than anyone, needs a safe haven. Give it a try, in a low-key, non-threatening way.

Families may face some common problems as they attempt to do dinner together. The following questions and answers may help.

What if Mom or Dad has to work late? Don't give up. There are a couple of ways to solve this dilemma. You could meet the working parent at a restaurant or a park on his or her way home, and share dinner together. Or if the boys are small and can't wait till Dad comes home to eat, serve their dinner early. When Dad sits down with you, serve them a bedtime snack at the family table.

How can I get the family talking? With some families this is no problem, but if it proves to be with yours, use some conversation starters. You and Dad look for little-known facts to share at dinner and the talk will follow. Soon the boys will be bringing their own fact-of-the-day to the table. Some families use a conversation jar that contains questions like "If you could be an animal, which one would you choose and why?" Take turns pulling slips of paper from the jar and see how the conversation takes off.

We've always had dinner together, and it seems a little routine. How can I spice things up? Change venues! Set a picnic outside or, better yet, set a picnic in the living room. Eat under the stars. Celebrate random events like Red Day where you all wear at least one red item to the table and eat as many red foods as you can. Fancy things up by getting out the candles and the china. Have a breakfast buffet at dinnertime. Or let Dad and the boys cook once a week.

Be sure to check the recommended reading list in appendix B for some great resources on strengthening family mealtimes. They're important times for your sons that will improve family communication.

One-on-One Talk

As our sons grow, opportunities crop up to have a special conversation—when they're entering middle school, when they've suffered a big disappointment, when they're leaving for college.

Before each of our sons took off for college, we took him out to eat alone. Yes, you'll have to make plans for the other boys, but it's an important and special time for a young man, and the occasion needs to be observed in a special way. Your college-bound son will see that you, too, realize it's an important passage for him and not just another family outing. If a meal out at a quiet restaurant is cost prohibitive, go to a park. Take a picnic lunch or cook something on a grill. Make it a time when you can talk freely with that one son.

Many families take everyone along when it's time to move a son into the dorm, but consider making this a parent-son occasion. I really questioned the value of this with our first son—I wanted everyone together, all the chicks in one nest, and I thought it would be good for the other boys. My husband felt our time would be better spent concentrated on one son than in corralling the others. The three younger boys stayed with friends and had a great time, and we did enjoy the time alone with our college freshman son. (The boys' farewell was tough enough at home—I can't imagine what it would have been like to drive away from the college campus with such sad brothers in the van!)

Don't underestimate the value of such talking times. Often it will seem like talking is the last thing your boys want to do at such times, so don't say, "Let's sit down and talk." Instead, come up with something special to do or somewhere special to go that will be conducive to conversation. Once he starts talking, here are some suggestions for you:

- Listen... all the way to the end. Don't jump into the middle of his talk.
- Be sure you understand what he's saying. Ask, if you need to, rephrasing what you think he said. "Do you mean that..."
- Be sure he understands what you're saying. With your preschool son, you may want to ask, "What did Mommy say?" Let him tell you what he perceived. If you ask your older son, "Do you know what I mean by that?" you may get only a nod, so a better question might be, "So, what do you think Mom is suggesting?"
- Show empathy for what he's experiencing. Don't always be quick to give solutions or try to fix things. Let him talk and explore the possibilities. When he's ready to hear from you, he'll ask what you think. If not, ask him if he wants to know what Mom thinks.

- Talk with him, talk with him, talk with him. Don't give up. Don't hound your son, of course, but do let him know you're there to talk, and you'd like nothing better than to engage him in conversation. Turn the music off and tune in to him.
- Let him know you love him, no matter what.

Don't buy into the "strong, silent type" myth, expecting your sons to suck up all emotion and never utter a word about how they feel. Kindlon and Thompson write in *Raising Cain* that when boys' feelings outstrip their language skills, they often turn to activity as an outlet, which can lead to aggressive behavior and classroom disruption.[7] Encourage your sons early on to talk about how they feel so they'll feel comfortable sharing with you and others as they mature.

Girl Talk

Mothers who have a daughter or two in the boy mix have a few things to consider. As stated earlier, as your son watches his mom and his sister communicate, he can learn valuable lessons. But if your daughters are more communicative than the boys in your household, it's easy to inadvertently neglect your sons for the more comfortable girl talk. You'll probably have to use different methods of communication with sons than you use with daughters, but don't give up on those boys.

Take an honest look at how you communicate with your sons and your daughters. In *Raising Cain*, Kindlon and Thompson cite studies suggesting that when a girl asks a question about emotions, she gets a longer explanation from Mom. If, for instance, she asks about a crying child, Mom may discuss possible reasons for the child's distress. This validates the daughter's inquiry into and discussion of emotions. If, on the other hand, a boy asks about a crying child, he's likely to be steered away from the subject with a quick, "I don't know. Now don't stare."

Thompson says such an answer is "less engaging, less infor-
mative and less rewarding for her son" and may communicate
that his discussion of emotions really isn't all that important.[8]
It's easy to feed the nurturing impulse of your daughter while
neglecting it in your son, but stand firm against surrendering to
the stereotypes.

Brother Talk

Encourage your sons to talk to their brothers. "Tyler has been
through that with his friend—ask him about it." "Mike did a
project like that for history, so why don't you talk to him?" Each
brother has a strength or experience that his brothers don't, and
encouraging them to go to one another allows each one to be the
expert on something.

This also fosters brother-to-brother communication, bringing them closer. They need to learn how to help one another,
and other communication lessons can be learned along the way.
Acting like the "know-it-all" doesn't go over well with brothers,
so a simple help session can turn into a lesson in how to communicate effectively.

Pave the way for good brother-to-brother communication
later in life by helping them remember each other at birthday
time and at Christmas. When your boys are young, handmade
gifts or items from the dollar store can suffice, and as they get
older, you can help them put more thought into gifts. One Christmas we took four boys under the age of ten to the dollar store
to choose one another's gifts. They had so much fun that day,
and later, opening each other's presents. It's time consuming to
help your sons create or buy cards for a brother on his birthday,
but it's a great habit to begin. It's particularly rewarding for you
later as they remember each other's birthdays when one is away
at college.

With the advent of cell phones, and especially texting, it's so
easy for them to contact each other as they grow up and leave

the nest. But that isn't likely to happen if you don't teach them to communicate while they're at home. (For more on maintaining that brother bond as they grow older, see chapter 9.)

Walking the Talk

As we stress communication, remember that we're training our sons for the future. They will need to communicate effectively on the job and in relationships. All that we do now paves the way for their success in those areas. In *Boys of Few Words*, Adam Cox, Ph.D., discusses the gap between boys' social and communication skills and the level that will be needed in the twenty-first century: "Now there are far fewer nonverbal, asocial lifestyle and vocational options. Your son is statistically unlikely to work the land or be a lonesome cowboy."[9] He makes the point that even technological jobs require skills in communication, and that communication in social realms—such as family—is a primary need. Cox writes that "helping [our sons] feel comfortable in communities of communication, where knowledge is gained through attentive interaction with others, is one of our primary jobs as parents."[10]

As Christian parents we have an even greater task because our sons' ultimate responsibilities as Christian men will likely include the leadership of families and the sharing of their faith. In 2 Corinthians 5:20 we're reminded that "We are therefore Christ's ambassadors, as though God were making his appeal through us." If our sons are to make an appeal on Christ's behalf, they will need to be communicators. As you take time out of your busy day to listen and to talk to your son, whether he's two or twelve, remember that you're laying a foundation for his future. So don't buy into the strong, silent stereotype, and don't give up. Talk on, Mom!

6

The Big O's—
Order and Organization

When a country is rebellious, it has many rulers,
but a man of understanding and knowledge
maintains order.

PROVERBS 28:2

Order and organization have two benefits—one is long-term and one is immediate. The opening verse refers to the long-term benefit. If we can teach our sons a bit of order and organization, it will help them maintain order in their adult lives, their families, and their work. The immediate advantage? Mom gets a little help around the house!

Notice I said a *little*. This isn't a chapter about getting your sons to clean the house for you; it's about teaching valuable skills. Erwin writes in *The Everything Parent's Guide to Raising Boys*, "If you believe you are teaching your son valuable skills, he is more likely to believe it, too. You are demonstrating love and commitment when you teach him to do things by himself and give him age-appropriate responsibilities."[1] In an age when an increasing number of adults over the age of twenty-five live at home with parents, equipping your son with the skills to be successful as an independent adult is crucial. Erwin writes, "Self esteem—a sense of one's worth and ability—grows out of skills and competency."[2] Wise moms teach valuable skills, bit by bit, from a boy's early years.

At times it may seem like a lot of work to teach them how to be organized. You know how it is—we all face the temptation to just do it ourselves because it seems easier. And just doing it yourself may be easier right now, but when your boys grow and their stuff accumulates and they bring bats, footballs, gloves, skates, and hockey sticks into the house and toss them anywhere, the clutter will get far beyond you. Unless you decide on a plan of action, your house will become a locker room—an unorganized one at that.

One of the most common problems with household organization is that adults organize with very little thought for the children. But if you involve your sons in the organizational process, your plans will make a lot more sense to them. They'll love buying into something they had a part in. Don't take it all on yourself, Mom—make it a group effort, and the family will become a team.

Organize, Schmorganize!

Why bother with organization? Orderliness in general makes everyone's lives easier, but organization can help your boys in some specific ways.

Organization teaches discipline. Boys learn there's a system for keeping order, and they learn the wherewithal to stick to it. In *Bringing Up Boys*, Dobson writes, "Boys need structure, they need supervision, they need to be civilized."[3] Structure and civilization are definitely by-products of organization.

Organization teaches self-control. Scripture tells us, "Like a city whose walls are broken down is a man who lacks self-control" (Prov. 25:28). Your sons will realize they can't just leave things where they want because they want to. Organization reminds us that other people in the household need to be considered.

Organization instills personal responsibility. If everyone in the family has a job to do, no matter how big or small, boys begin to see themselves as a valuable part of the family.

Organization prepares our sons to be leaders. What picture pops into your mind when you think of a leader? Not a man surrounded by chaos, I'm sure. We're raising boys to be dads and bosses and co-workers, and we need to equip them now to lead later. God's promises for those who lead are laid out in Daniel 12:3: "Those who are wise will shine like the brightness of the heavens, and those who lead many to righteousness, like the stars forever and ever." Equip your sons to be leaders.

Organization helps boys escape the helpless men stereotype. It's not uncommon today for young men to wait until their later twenties to marry. That means they'll live alone for a while after college and, frankly, they need to be able to take care of themselves. *Organization will help your boys help you, and they'll learn from that.* If you raise your sons like princes, they'll never understand what it takes to keep a household running. If they share in the load, they'll have a sense of what that entails. They'll also develop a sense of helping others, and they'll feel part of a team effort.

Before we launch into the specifics of this chapter, let me remind moms of one thing: Just because your children are boys doesn't mean they don't need to learn how to organize and help around the house. Those boys will one day be doing their own laundry, and learning household skills *while* they're learning how to pay the bills and hold down a job will just make their lives that much harder. And organization isn't all about housework. Organization involves keeping your stuff together and being able to find what you need when you need it. Everyone needs that skill. The good news is that if you reinforce a sense of organization with your toddler, it won't be a foreign concept when he's twelve. Not only that, his wife will thank you for it one day!

The ABC's of the Big O's

We're all at different points in the marathon of parenting, but you can still lay a foundation for family organization. Some of you already have three boys at home while other moms may have one toddler with another boy on the way. So where do you start? Organize yourself. The best teacher models what she's trying to teach, so take this time to get yourself organized. Here are three things I've found to be invaluable in setting a foundation for family organization.

1. Use a wall calendar. List doctor appointments, games, practices, school project due dates, and so forth. Get in the habit of saying, "I'm putting it on the calendar" and once they're old enough, let them do it. I must admit, the calendar came in very handy with Boy #4. By this time I was so busy with boys ages 9, 6, and 3 that I didn't have time to fill out his baby book. I used the calendar, recording his weight after a doctor appointment and even noting when teeth came in. Later, when things settled down, I transferred the notes to his baby book.

2. Establish a grocery list. A magnetic board that sticks to your refrigerator is perfect. I list groceries down one side and discount store items on the other. This has helped me to organize my shopping and to be sure I get what we need. As the boys have grown, they've used it, too. They've learned that when they open the last package of hot dogs or if they notice we're down to half a loaf of bread, they should write it on the board. That way they take some responsibility and it helps Mom, too. Use of the board creates not only responsibility, but some positive brother peer pressure: "We're out of hot dogs? Okay, who opened the last package and didn't write it on the board?"

3. Plan ahead. If something crazy is going to happen in a houseful of boys, it's not going to be on a lazy summer afternoon when there's nothing going on. Chaos characteristically ensues when you're getting ready to leave the house for church, already ten minutes late. And you're ten minutes late because boys were searching for shoes and belts. Every Saturday night of my mom-life has been spent getting boys' clothes ready for Sunday. Enough can go wrong on Sunday morning, and getting some things ready the night before can relieve some of the stress. When my boys wore dress shirts, you'd find me pressing those on Saturday night and hanging them where they could reach them. Sunday shoes would be laid out with socks and belts on Saturday night. Part of your family Saturday night ritual can be to gather what's needed for Sunday and put it all where it needs to be. Teach your boys to gather and organize, and the family will be acting as a team.

The Winning Team

In *Raising Sons Without Fathers*, authors Terdal and Kennedy suggest these techniques for single mothers to help make their sons successful at accomplishing their chores:

- Break down tasks into the fewest basic steps.
- Adapt your standards. Don't expect perfection.
- Set priorities. Decide which jobs should be done when.
- Structure the environment so they can reach needed items.
- Decide on rewards and consequences ahead of time.
- Be very specific.[4]

These ideas ring true for any mother of boys, whether or not a dad is in the picture.

Help! The Garbage Truck Is Coming!

Work together as you decide who will be responsible for what task. Will one boy take out the trash on one day and another the recycling? What will each boy be responsible for on his own? Start by asking each son, "What can *you* do?" Whatever responsibilities you set, the system will work only if you hold them accountable. We set up a chart in the computer with each boy's name and task. It was the job of the oldest boy to print next week's chart on Saturday night, and it was mounted on the refrigerator. Each boy checked off his jobs every night before bed. Some moms use a small dry-erase board in each child's room, where the children can write their own jobs each week. Decide what will work for you and stick to it.

One mom I know uses a Room Patrol system. Each boy is assigned an area he's responsible for, and that child checks out his area before bed. He has the authority to remind his brothers if they've left anything there that belongs to them. In our home, backpacks and shoes were kept in our front hall against the wall. One boy had the responsibility to straighten the shoes, and all of the boys had "backpack ready for school" on their charts. Homework, permission slips, books, had to be packed away and ready so in the morning they had to grab only their lunches.

Keeping boys accountable for their jobs ensures the work gets done, but it has other benefits, too. It doesn't take long for them to see that if they fail to take out the trash and the garbage truck is coming, someone else has to do it. Boys begin to see that a family is a team. When one son has a camping trip or will be away and can't fulfill his responsibilities, don't solve the problem for him. Instead, encourage the boys to figure out a way to get those things done. If they want to swap jobs with another brother for that week, let the boys mediate that.

One morning we drove off for school and saw the garbage truck driving into the neighborhood. One of the boys realized he'd neglected to put the trash out. Knowing his dad was still at home, my son asked, "Could you call Dad and ask him to get the trash to the curb for me?" I said, "No, but you can" and handed him my cell phone. Give your sons responsibility for their responsibilities. Our desire is to see our sons grow to be faithful men, for Scripture tells us, "A faithful man will be richly blessed" (Prov. 28:20).

Legos, Action Figures, and Socks

Yes, I know how it is with toddlers—toys all over the house. When our boys were young, the family room became the play room. It was connected to the kitchen and right by the washer and dryer so I could cook and do laundry while I could hear and see what was happening. If I was needed to referee, I was close at hand, and I could take a "play break" with the boys whenever I wanted. Confining the toy clutter to one room helped tremendously. I could go into the living room, sit on the couch, and pretend the rest of my house looked like that, for just a few minutes. I've heard mothers say they let a child play with only one thing at a time, making him put something back before getting something else out. The creative side of me, though, always screamed, "No!" After all, how can you test that Lego roadway if you can't get the little cars out? And maybe that little toy man and his family will fit into the truck—but how will you know if you can play with only one at a time?

My alternative to that was Playtime Pickup. All the toys were kept in the family room except for a few special things. My décor in those days was Early American Family. I figured, *Why fight it?* But whenever we left the house, ate lunch, or took a nap, we'd pick up toys. Putting toys away a couple of times a day reinforced that everything has a home and needs to be there. We had bins for everything—a crate for the big vehicles, a bucket for little people, boxes for the Legos, places for books and puzzles. When it was pickup time, toys went back in those places. At bedtime, the same activity took place.

Doing that was great because, first of all, when I walked into the room I could actually see the carpet. Most of all, though, it instilled a routine for the boys. At times a special construction project was in process, and it would be left in place—but everything around it was picked up. As the boys got older, they kept more toys in their rooms, and one of their jobs on their charts was always "floor cleared at night." When they graduated to spending more time in their own rooms, they had responsibility for their own space and were held accountable for it.

Sorting toys into their proper places is a great foundational tool for little ones, so exercising it at other times, as long as it's not too complicated, is good for them. Three- and four-year-olds, for example, can sort socks. Even just separating all the clean socks—whites from colors—is a sorting exercise for little ones. When I took all four boys to the grocery store, I'd often give the older ones a mission—get whole milk, find the cereal. We'd place things in the cart in some organized fashion and bag it the same way. Heavy things together, frozen things together, soft stuff together.

Bats, Gloves, and Underwear

How many bats and gloves do you need? I'm sure far less than you have in your house! How to manage those? If you have a garage or a porch, relegate certain things to the outside. We initialed tall plastic bins for each boy to store his sports equipment in. Baseball gloves and other equipment were labeled with their initials as well so they didn't get them mixed up.

With multiple boys, labeling is a wonderful thing. If you can buy underwear and socks of differing brands that's great, but it you can't, labeling makes laundry sorting go a lot faster. I used a permanent marker to put a red dot on one of my boys clothing so I could easily distinguish his from the boy closest in size. If those clothes were passed down, the dot was changed to an initial for the next brother. When you have more than one boy, clothes get passed down a time or two, and sometimes it's hard to remember who's wearing that shirt now.

When they shared rooms, the boys had different sides of the dresser and each took one half of the closet. Shoes and other personal items had to be lined up under "your side." In order to hand off some clothing responsibility to the boys, I placed a basket outside each door for clean clothes. Once I placed their clean clothes in the basket, they moved them inside the room into the correct drawer. Each boy had a bin in his room for dirty laundry, and I kept a bin for dirty darks and one for dirty lights in the laundry room. They sorted and deposited their laundry into those bins, so it was easy for me to tell at a glance which needed to be done right away. And those awful, smelly athletic uniforms and workout clothes? The boys learned early how to do that kind of laundry.

Paper—An Organizational Nightmare

Children bring home paper from church, from school, from club meetings, and athletics—and it seems to multiply. Some is important (forms to sign and return), some is informational, some is great for the memory box, and some is just paper. The trick is in deciding which is which and what to do with it. I know one mom who has a file folder on the counter for each child. When they get home, the kids put papers in their files. Before bed, Mom checks and signs forms that need to be signed or reads important information. My boys would always deal with those kinds of papers when they did their homework or packed up backpacks. Find a consistent method that works for you and stick to it.

What about that wonderful memory stuff? I have big plastic bins for each boy—notes, special cards, special papers, and pictures go in those. If you're a scrapbooking mom, all those paper memories will be sorted for you when you find time to scrapbook. If not, maybe your son's wife will someday enjoy the contents of the bin and put a scrapbook together for him. But if you have multiple boys, storing it now in separate bins for each makes a lot more sense than plowing through it later. You can't keep everything, so try taking pictures of your son with that great Lego creation or the science fair exhibit. I have no room to keep that science fair tri-fold board, but I have some wonderful pictures of Andrew standing by it with his ribbon. He'll get a kick out of that photo someday when he's older.

3, 2, 1, Launch

Everything moms do to train our sons helps get them ready to launch out beyond the home. Training in organization, though, will be particularly helpful. As they grow and acquire more responsibilities, they'll need a different type of help in organizing. When our eldest son got his first job, we took him to the bank to get an account set up. He began receiving bank statements, and soon information about SATs, ACTs, and colleges began to fill the mailbox, and the piles of paper grew. We started a portable file box system for each son, working together on the categories. We began with a place for all the categories mentioned above, and then we added in each box a file for each college that was under consideration. All correspondence from that college went into the file, and SAT scores were filed in their proper place, too. As acceptance letters and scholarship offers came in, they went in the file also.

Once a son chose his school and readied himself for college, we reviewed the file categories once again. Our son needed his social security card and passport at school, so categories were created for personal documents. Now he needed categories for paperwork on college loans, work information, FAFSA and financial aid, and car information. Armed with his file box, he went off to college. I can't say we didn't get a panicked call once in a while: "Dad, where's my social security card?" At least we knew we could say, "Son, it was in your file box when you left home. Check there."

Without a system, it's too easy for important documents to get buried in a dorm room under piles of paper and laundry. The file box worked for our sons. We began working with our sons and their file boxes when they were about age fifteen, and each box got reorganized into different categories several times before college. At least each son had some training in organization and left home with a good sense of how to keep track of important things.

Routine + Flexibility = Organization

In a family, both routine and flexibility are important. First, let's consider routine. Routine makes young children feel safe because they know what's coming and what is expected of them. Snack time means, for instance, bedtime is ten minutes away. At bedtime, Mom will read one story, they'll sing one song, and pray before getting tucked in. When it was Dad's turn to attend to snacks and bedtime, my husband heard probably a thousand times, "That isn't the way Mommy does it!" Continuity, though, helps the kids and helps Mom and Dad. Life is so much easier if the kids know that eight o'clock is bedtime so that fight is not fought each night.

The danger is when routine becomes rigidity. Special occasions call for some deviation from the routine, and we need to be willing to go with the flow sometimes. And sometimes it's time to adjust what we've considered the norm. As boys grow and have more homework, or work and athletic schedules encroach on their time, their needs change. Other times, it becomes obvious that some aspect of our family organization just isn't working. Maybe it's time to sit down as a family and say, "What can we do to make this happen?" Not only does that focus the family on the need, but it allows all of the boys to share in the resolution. Getting your sons' input on the problem lets them be part of the answer.

Remember the beginning of this chapter? Organization teaches discipline, self-control, and personal responsibility. When we teach our sons organizational skills, we help equip them for the future. They learn to take care of themselves, to be part of a team, and to help others. What better training for leadership could there be?

7

Media in a Young Man's Life

I am sending you out like sheep among wolves. Therefore be as shrewd as snakes and as innocent as doves.

MATTHEW 10:16

Christ advised His disciples to be "as shrewd as snakes and as innocent as doves." How can our sons benefit from that advice? As they enter the wolves' territory of the outside world, they'll need a healthy balance of innocence and shrewdness, and that's where moms and dads come in. Parents need to agree on strategy and parameters, but Mom is many times on the front line in this media war because she's usually the purchaser for her young sons, and she's at home when Johnny wants to pick up a book or pop in a movie.

There's no doubt that our society is becoming increasingly media-oriented. This is an age when to "friend" someone has taken on a completely new meaning, and often our sons are faced with electronic choices we never had to make. Although the opportunity to connect with vast amounts of useful information can be positive, there's a glut of data and images at our sons' fingertips that is useless, immoral, and harmful. And its allure is appealing, especially to our sons. Why is that?

- Media is visual, and so are our sons. Its messages are swift and powerful.
- Media preference is tied to peer pressure. "Everybody is talking about that movie!"
- Technology is fast. Download that movie in minutes. Who wants to wait?
- With technology, the user is in control. He makes the choice whether to click that icon or how to build his army in a video game.

- Computer life lacks the complication of real relationships. Don't like that person? Just don't "friend" them, or choose not to reply. It's not like they're standing in front of your son, waiting for him to answer. He can interact on any level he chooses, and it's easy to disconnect from real, skin-and-bone relationships.

The allure of media is clear, and its power is strong. It can be used for good, but only when we parents actively involve ourselves in our sons' media diet.

Media Time

Media grows to be a monster only when we feed it too much, and that's what many of today's children are doing. Dr. Meg Meeker reports on the findings of the Kaiser Family Foundation: "In an average week, a boy spends 45½ hours (or more time than he would spend at a full-time job) with either television, computer, music or MP3s," while his weekly total for physical activity is roughly one quarter of that. In addition, the average boy will spend well less than half the time with his parents that he spends with his media.[1] Meeker feels a mother's job is to be a filter for her son, setting ground rules and insisting that computers and televisions be used communally, for the family. Meeker reminds us, "There are many influences you can't prevent, but what comes into your home you most certainly can."[2]

The Problem of Control

We can't let society dictate our standards; we need to take control of the use of media in our own homes. Technology choices for our sons are personal choices, and that includes the use of cell phones. Mom and Dad must decide when the time is right for their son to own a cell phone. And once that decision has been made, parents need to consider other things like a phone's capabilities and its applications. So much can be accessed and downloaded on today's phones that parents are wise to take time as they make personal cell phone decisions.

Texting is one activity that can easily overtake family interaction, as your son texts back and forth with friends during conversation, family mealtime, or study time. A friend of mine has a bin for cell phones at her home. The phones go into the bin during meals, until homework is completed, and at bedtime. The phones don't live in her sons' pockets or in their rooms, so their intrusion into family life is minimal. Some families have only a car cell. It serves as a link between driving teens and Mom and Dad, but it stays in the car. There are many wise ways to handle cell phone usage in your family. Be creative and take time as you make choices that are right for your sons.

Limits and *balance* are great concepts for your sons to learn as you weigh media and technology choices. Ecclesiastes 3:1 tells us "there is a time for everything," and 1 Corinthians 6:12 tells us that "not everything is beneficial." Our sons need to learn to balance media wisely. A good rule of thumb is that family time means video games and phones off and ear buds out. Believe it or not, even with a house of four boys, we've never owned a video gaming system. We used computer games and limited each son's time on the computer. (It's interesting to hear what the older ones say about that now. See chapter 10, "A Word from the Boys," for their take on a childhood without video games.)

Foster Discernment, Not Spoon-Feeding

You can't control what your sons are exposed to at school, in a friend's home, or in a number of other situations. So how do we help our sons navigate the world of media choices? We teach them to discern. When we begin teaching discernment early, ours sons may grow into young men who can make wise choices themselves.

British novelist E. M. Forster wrote, "Spoon feeding in the long run teaches us nothing but the shape of the spoon." We want our sons to leave our homes with so much more. Parents who spoon-feed their children say things like, "No, we're not watching that. Just because." Or maybe, "Turn that off. I'm not listening to that liberal nonsense." "You want to watch something on PBS? Are you kidding?"

Let's talk about age-appropriateness a moment. Before children reach the age where they can think critically, their choices need to be made for them. But once they can reason and express themselves logically, we need to help guide them safely through the media waters by teaching them to discern. It is, in fact, our responsibility. If we ignore the impact of media, refusing to engage our children in biblical discussions about the images and ideas they encounter every day, we're guilty of spiritual neglect.

This is not just Mom's responsibility, of course. (See appendix A for "Dad's Part in All of This.") Both parents need to be in agreement as they teach discernment. But in a household of boys, Mom often encounters media preferences she doesn't share, and she has to be equipped to relate to those. Most moms holding this book would not list *Braveheart* or *Rudy* on their top ten movie list! *Little Women* may speak to you, but chances are that *Lord of the Flies* will have a stronger impact on your sons. Mom has to purposefully tune in to the media that attracts boys, both for good and ill.

Even if you choose your sons' books and movies while they're under your roof, the opportunity will still arise for them to make their own choices. Even if you never purchase video games and keep your sons away from violent gaming, they'll visit a friend outfitted with games you've shunned. When that happens, if they've learned to discern, they'll have in place a set of spiritual and moral guidelines that will help govern their choices.

Reading Is the Perfect Tool

Reading is a great place to begin teaching discernment. Many mothers will read to their sons before they'll plop them in front of the television, and that's a good thing. When reading to your young son, stop and ask questions like,

- Why do you think Thomas felt that way?
- Did Morris make the right choice there?
- Why is Harold's mom unhappy with him?

These are thought-provoking questions that lead a child to examine the story and the actions of the character. When you ask these kinds of questions about what you're reading, you're giving your son the opportunity to express what he understands about the story. Doing that creates a great foundation, for your son knows he can trust you with what he thinks about a story, and you've created a teachable moment. There's no iron-clad guarantee that when your son is a teen he'll talk to you about moral choices as he watches 24. But if you lay the groundwork early, your son will get used to thinking about what a story is really trying to communicate. It won't seem odd, then, when he's a teen, for him to sit down to discuss a movie's theme with you.

Reading is not only a great first avenue to introduce discernment to your sons, but it's the perfect avenue. To discern is to perceive the true nature of something, to cut through outward issues to get to the truth. Jonathan Rogers, author of the Wilderking Trilogy, a fantasy-adventure series reminiscent of Narnia, says that "story is truer than precept." The story of the prodigal son can be boiled down to grace and forgiveness, but "it's the story that does the work on us, not the disembodied precept.... You can talk about grace until you're blue in the face, but you aren't going to come up with a definition that improves on the parable of the Prodigal Son: a father, arms outstretched, welcoming a rebellious and wicked son back into his home."[3]

A reader is an understander—he knows what it's like to be in someone else's shoes. What more could we ask for our sons? Rogers says, "A well-written book allows them to experience what it's like to be another person. And isn't that the very basis of empathy and kindness? Isn't it a key component of love?"[4] Story moves us, whether we're four, fourteen, or forty. Tales make us think big as they take us into a world of adventure or fantasy where exciting things can happen. Good stories inspire boys and give them perspective on other people, on what matters, on what is true.

Lay a Foundation for Reading

How can moms set the stage so that good stories can do their work on our sons? Encourage them to read! Here are some ideas:

- Read to them, no matter what their ages. Infants and toddlers love the attention and the lap time, not to mention the stories. I teach high school sophomores who love for me to read to them using lots of inflection and voices.
- Let them see you read. You or your husband may not be big fiction readers, but just let them see you reading something. The newspaper, your Bible, magazines.
- Emphasize the value of reading. All of us need to have reading skills, no matter what our line of work. There will always be instruction manuals to follow and e-mails to read. But more importantly, we know from Psalm 119:11 that reading Scripture is essential for Christians. The psalmist declared, "I have hidden your word in my heart that I might not sin against you."
- Provide different types of reading. Many boys, especially as they get older, will abandon stories and turn to nonfiction. Some boys' interest in reading can be sparked by a subscription to a special interest magazine.
- Listen to a book on CD together or age-appropriate radio dramas like Focus on the Family's *Adventures in Odyssey*. Topics or characters they hear about can spark further investigation into a book.

- Provide age-appropriate reading that has a high interest level for your boys. Don't expect them at age seven to read the college-age classics or to immerse themselves in a story about two girls. Look for interesting reading for boys. If you need some ideas, check out the resource section in appendix B.

Adam Cox asks a telling question in *Boys of Few Words*: "Dollar for dollar, do you spend as much on books for your son as you spend on videos and computer games? An intellectually impoverished home has a tower of DVDs and no bookshelf."[5]

The Reluctant Reader

"But," you say, "my son is not a reader. He'd rather be playing baseball or riding his bike." Sigmund Brouwer, author of a number of high-interest series for boys, says the problem may be your unrealistic expectations. Boys like action, and of course your boy enjoys those activities. But there's good news. "Boys, in general," says Brouwer, "like action stories. Sports. True adventure. Cars. Outdoors. All the things boys like in real life, they will like in books and magazines."[6]

But boys face a crucial transition time around the second grade, when they progress from picture books to short chapter books. The lack of "boy titles" available in short chapter books means that boys have fewer choices to interest them. Practice makes perfect—or at least makes one better—and if boys don't have much choice in books to practice on, their reading skills are going to suffer. The lack of choices in boy books doesn't get any better as they get older, and their skills continue to lag behind. By fifth or sixth grade, boys have no desire to do what they're not good at, and pressure from teachers is escalating because as they get older, reading for content increases.

So if you have a young son who is a reluctant reader, look for books that will interest him. High-interest, low-vocabulary books are usually shorter, fast-paced, and won't intimidate boys who are not skilled at reading. These books, says Brouwer, can provide a "stepping stone to make up for all the lack of practice during crucial reading years in grades two and three." Brouwer suggests a simple three-step test to determine if a book is right for your reluctant reader:

1. If the back cover description is appealing, go to step two. If not, look for another title.
2. Read the first chapter aloud together. If it doesn't grab the boy's interest in the first ten pages, set this book aside. If it does, go on to step three.
3. Read any page in the middle of the book. If the boy finds five words he doesn't understand, pass on it. Assure him that practice will make this book possible later and, like a good friend, it will wait for him.

If the book passes all three tests, Brouwer says, "you can promise your reluctant reader it will be as much fun as watching a movie."[7]

Speaking of Movies (and Television)...

The techniques we've discussed for dialoguing about books will work just as well for movies. And in movies, the combination of visual images with the power of story makes a big impression on our sons. Remember, though, that your average Hollywood producer is trying to make a profit. He figures it's your job to teach your sons about what's right and wrong. A movie-maker's values and worldview may be totally different from yours. When a movie combines the power of story with a certain set of values, the end result can be a powerful message that flies in the face of your values. It's our job to pick through the glut to find the real goods, and then to teach our sons to do the same.

Your standards will likely differ from the standards of other parents, and that may be a point of contention. So, especially if your son spends time at his friend's house, it's best to keep the lines of communication open with other parents. Let other parents know what your standards are and ask them to help your son abide by those while he's visiting. Do remember to weigh your choices by your standards, not by another's. Several books in the Reading, Media, and Technology section in appendix B contain recommendations for books or movies. Not every book and movie they recommend will pass muster with every one of you who is reading this book. There is much to weigh as you make media choices. No matter what society tells you, it's your job to decide what your children read, watch, and listen to.

Early Exposure to TV and Movies

In *Unplug Your Kids*, David Dutwin reports the American Academy of Pediatrics' suggestion that children under age two not watch any television. The AAP further recommends that older children not watch more than one or two hours of television or video a day. Nonviolent and educational programming is recommended for children, and the AAP states that most of all, television should not be used as a substitute for activities like playing, exercising, or reading. The wide range of educational videos today can help parents make proper choices for their young ones, but it's important to remember that AAP's recommendation is that children under age two not watch any television.[8]

As our children reach school age, the television competes with school work, reading, and family time. How can we harness the power of TV in our families and use it wisely? Here are a few ideas:

- Set a good example. Don't leave the TV on all the time. Be discerning about what you watch. Don't watch programs that aren't age-appropriate for your sons before they are in bed (and asleep).

- Turn off the TV at dinner time!
- Keep the television in a central location. That way you can monitor its usage and be a part of viewing with your sons.
- Make conversation a family priority. It should take precedence over any television show.
- Homework should be completed before the TV is turned on.
- Talk about the difference between what is real on television and what is not. This includes advertising. Younger children especially have a hard time discerning truth from sales talk.
- Plan your viewing. Look at the viewing guide and decide what the family will watch together instead of cruising all around the spectrum, exposing your sons to all kinds of images.
- Invest in a good book about media and children. *Unplug Your Children* by David Dutwin examines the effects of media on children at different ages and gives specific guidelines for different age groups.
- Stick with your bedtime rituals. Don't delay bedtime or shortcut on reading and singing and prayer together so your son can catch a few extra minutes of some show. Turn it off—that's what recorders are for.

The University of Michigan Health System Web site quotes Nancy W. Dickey, M.D., past president of the American Medical Association: "A good question to ask in every household—if a child (or an adult) wasn't watching TV, what else could he or she be doing?"[9] Psalm 90:12 reminds us of how quickly time passes and to use that time wisely: "Teach us to number our days aright, that we may gain a heart of wisdom."

Finding Gold Amidst the Dross

Yes, there's gold to be found in movies. You just have to do your homework. A mom's first step is to realize that movies are often made to create wealth for Hollywood, to advance a certain agenda, or to create merchandising opportunities. That puts the responsibility for monitoring your sons' choices squarely on your and Dad's shoulders—and you'll both need to be the enforcer. How do you approach this treasure hunt?

- Talk to your sons about negative influences. Explain why they can't watch a certain movie or television show. Be sure they understand it's not "just because I said so," but it's because the content is harmful for their heart and spirit. Let them know you love them too much to give them what can hurt them.
- Talk about what you *do* watch. (For young viewers, see "Early Exposure to TV and Movies" above.)
- Talk about what you believe, what you hold dear, and why.
- Look for stories that build the kind of character you want to see in your sons. Use the media for *your* purposes—to teach character. (Several books listed in appendix B give summaries of books and movies that will help you choose.)

Take the recommendations in appendix B, though, with a grain of salt. Not all parents and psychologists share your same standards, so don't take every recommendation as a full endorsement. You're the parent—it's up to you to make personal decisions regarding your family, so preview items before handing them to your sons.

With an Eye to the News

The news can be a great launching point for discussion with your sons, but again, keep an eye on age-appropriateness. Our sons span nine years, so we had a hard time ever watching the news all together. I remember specifically when we got home after school on September 11, 2001. We just could not let our younger sons watch the images that crossed the television screen that day, and after a while, we told the older boys they'd seen enough. We began to realize that we had to moderate even our own viewing. More is not always better. Sometimes as parents, we have the responsibility of deciding how much truth about the fallen world our children can bear. Here are some hints for handling the news with your sons:

- Make discussion about current events a normal thing for your sons. Keep the newspaper handy, share it at breakfast or waiting to load up for school, and be ready to talk about what's happening in the world.
- Put news in its proper perspective. Discussing how something may be an isolated incident will help relieve fears your sons may have.
- Contrast the news source with another that has a different worldview. Television news may be coming from a more liberal perspective than you espouse, and watching it offers the perfect opportunity to talk about the differences.
- Watch the news *with* your boys. And have the remote ready in case you need to mute an inappropriate or disturbing story—or turn the program off.
- Discuss what your family would do in a particular situation like a natural disaster, or what your family can do to help.

Considering the Family Mix

I mentioned that our sons span nine years, and that did present some problems. If you have sons who are old enough to handle the news or some age-appropriate show or movie, make sure they don't view those while the younger boys are around. Our sons' age span made it particularly difficult to choose a movie all would enjoy. But there are bigger lessons to be learned here. Your older sons play the role of the protector for their younger brothers, and it's good to remind them of that. The older boys may need to tape something and watch it later, after the younger ones are in bed, but a little waiting never hurt anyone. All of your sons can get the message that Mom and Dad are doing what's right for all the boys right now.

If you have older sons or teens and are just now beginning to monitor their media, you may find the process a bit rocky. Families who have watched or read and talked together all along will find discussion about discernment to be a natural progression as their sons enter the teen years. Those who haven't may find their sons resistant: *What does it matter what I watch? Why do we have to talk about it?*

You can forestall some of that reluctance by making movie night special—a real family time. Decide together on a movie to rent, make popcorn, and enjoy a night together. Maybe take an intermission to load up on popcorn again, and talk about what you've seen so far. As you do, ask thought-provoking questions that will encourage your sons to examine their own beliefs and then see how those situations play out in the story. As you discuss the story, compare the action to biblical principles. How can this teach your sons to discern?

- They'll learn what kinds of questions to ask about the media they want to use.
- They'll learn how to compare their answers to biblical principles.
- They'll take these lessons with them as they leave the nest, and they'll be much more likely to travel safely among the wolves.

If you have a girl in the mix, a rose among the thorns, you'll have to teach respect for one another's preferences—and that's a valuable lesson for life. The boys won't enjoy *Cinderella*, and she may not take to the story of Davy Crockett, but your sons and daughters can learn to show respect for each other's likes and dislikes. Strive for balance, Mom, be fair, and expect the same from them. That way your daughters as well as your sons will leave home with a sense of self-worth and the worth of others. They'll understand that everyone's preferences need to be respected, and will learn to compromise in areas of entertainment and recreation—and perhaps in other areas as well.

Take Heart, Mom

Maneuvering through the world of media isn't easy, no matter what your sons' ages. There will be hills to climb and pitfalls to avoid as you endeavor to teach your sons to discern. But take heart in the fact that you're not alone on this obstacle course. Your desire to see your sons grow into godly men comes from above, as does your help. Second Chronicles 16:9 serves as a great reminder: "For the eyes of the LORD range throughout the earth to strengthen those whose hearts are fully committed to him."

8

Growing Respect

Show proper respect to everyone: Love the brotherhood of believers, fear God, honor the king.

1 PETER 2:17

Planting the seeds of respect and nurturing their growth is one of a mom's most important tasks. Respect is at the core of a healthy self-image, and it's crucial to strong relationships. Parents can cultivate respect in their sons when the boys are very young. As you water and nurture those seeds of respect through modeling and teaching, you'll be preparing your sons for future relationships at home, among peers, at work, and with their Creator. As you grow a healthy respect in your boys for themselves and others and a proper understanding of authority, you'll lay a foundation also for healthy dating and marriage relationships.

Raising Sons That People Like to Be Around

Early in the parenting marathon I decided I wanted my sons not to be children that people dreaded, but children whom adults liked to be around. I figured it would make life easier for everyone if that were the case, and it would teach my boys some important lessons in the process. Adults generally don't mind being in the presence of children who show respect. Treating others with respect is an important, lifelong social skill, but more than that, respect is an attitude. Respect says, "All of us are born with worth, and I acknowledge your value." Treating people with disrespect discounts their value. Titus 3:1–2 gives a complete definition of true respect: "Remind the people to be subject to rulers and authorities, to be obedient, to be ready to do whatever is good, to slander no one, to be peaceable and considerate, and to show true humility toward all men."

Our goal as moms is to raise sons who can navigate independently through life and show true humility without reminders. We won't always be by their sides to say, "Be nice," or "Listen when others speak to you." If they acquire the attitude of respect early, they'll be able to avoid many difficult situations. And even more importantly, as Christians, we have so much more reason to show respect to others. Since we are "Christ's ambassadors, as though God were making his appeal through us" (2 Cor. 5:20), our witness should be winsome. Others should look at the way we handle life's ups and downs and take notice. If a Christ-like respect lies at the back of our actions and reactions, the world will take note. We want the world to see our sons respecting authority, respecting themselves, and respecting others.

Respecting Authority

Respect is not the same as obedience. Many times children obey out of fear of consequences. When children obey not out of fear but out of respect, they're saying, "I'm going to obey you because I value you. I trust you and know that you want what's best for me." That's the attitude we want to instill in our sons.

Respect for authority grows ultimately from a surrender to our Creator, the ultimate authority. When our sons understand that the guidelines and precepts in the Bible are there for their good, because of divine love for them, they live out respect to those around them. And respect for governmental and school authority flows from that same understanding.

Respecting Themselves

Our sons must know their own value, their own worth. Even when they're young, we begin teaching them to take care of themselves. They learn the value of eating well, getting enough sleep, brushing their teeth. As we teach such lessons, we show we value them, and our boys begin to see their intrinsic worth.

As our sons get older, they must respect themselves enough not to get caught up in things that could be harmful to them. If they can see their bodies as vessels for God's use, they'll be living that respect daily. Romans 12:1 tells us, "Therefore, I urge you brothers, in view of God's mercy, to offer your bodies as living sacrifices, holy and pleasing to God—this is your spiritual act of worship." As we use Scripture to teach our sons about those behaviors that are unhealthy and unacceptable, we underscore respect for their Maker and communicate their own self-worth. A proper view of worth—theirs and others—is essential to forming strong relationships.

Respecting Others

In our fast-paced, me-first world, we don't see a lot of respect for others; it's sorely needed today. A healthy respect for others won't happen without respect for authority and for oneself. Respect for others begins at home and extends into school and the playground. As children grow, that respect permeates their peer and dating relationships. As adults, that same sense of respect makes them more likely to be happy, successful employees and employers, and loving fathers and spouses. Listen to the praise from Proverbs for a trustworthy worker: "Like the coolness of snow at harvest time is a trustworthy messenger to those who send him; he refreshes the spirit of his masters" (Prov. 25:13). The trustworthy messenger shows respect for himself and those around him. What a winsome witness in a me-first world!

Being the Model Parent

It's been said that children learn only 5 percent from direct instruction, and 95 percent from modeling. That places the ball squarely in the parental court. Our sons see us deal with grumpy cashiers, annoying telemarketers, and unfair situations every day. What do they see? Imagine little eyes watching you. Here are a few questions to ask yourself:

- How do you react when treated rudely by a store clerk?
- What's your reaction when someone cuts you off in traffic?
- What do you say after you hang up from your fifth telemarketer in an hour?
- How do you handle it when you've been wronged (given too little change or the incorrect item)?
- What do you say when your son complains that he doesn't like a teacher's rules?
- How do you correct your son when he misbehaves in public? Do you publicly berate him?

All of these situations have the potential to teach respect or disrespect for others. Remember the admonition in James 1:19 to be "quick to listen, slow to speak and slow to become angry"? When you're treated rudely, don't respond in kind.

In a me-first world, let your children see you place someone else's needs first. Who knows what that clerk is facing today? Maybe your kind treatment will be a small ray of sunshine in her or his otherwise gloomy day. What good does it do to berate someone who cut you off in traffic? A much better lesson for your children would be to explain how that behavior creates a dangerous driving situation. Your children will notice and admire your forbearance when you tell that telemarketer kindly but firmly, "Please remove us from your calling list." When you or your child has been wronged, you don't have to cower and ignore the situation, but handle these circumstances with respect. My mother always used to say, "You catch more flies with honey than vinegar"—and she was right!

Here are some tips for modeling respect that will increase the likelihood of seeing the same behaviors in your grown sons:

- *Listen.* When you ask your sons about their day or the game or their latest adventure, stop and listen to their response. In an age of multi-tasking, we often find ourselves less and less physically connected to the one we're communicating with. Make a conscious effort to make eye contact with your son, to reach out and pat him on the back, or give him a quick hug as you talk. When you take time to really connect, you're showing his value.

- *Be positive.* Not all his news will be positive, but look for the up side. If one thing didn't go so well, look for successes elsewhere. When he admits defeat, don't belittle him— build him up. Remember to "encourage one another and build each other up" (1 Thess. 5:11). Let your son know that he's too valuable to let this one defeat get him down.

- *Be honest.* Respect your son enough not to build false hope in him; that can lead to bitterness. He needs to know his strengths and weaknesses, and he should be encouraged realistically. Even though he may not be drafted into the majors, he can still learn lessons of commitment and perseverance, and enjoy the camaraderie of sports. Encourage him not to give up even if he isn't the best; use the situation to help him know himself and learn bigger lessons.

- *Be consistent.* You and Dad need to provide a united front or the boys will chip away at the boundaries. Don't waffle on things; we respect consistency in others.

- *Let them know you love them.* Yes, even as they grow up, they need to hear "I love you," and they need a mom's hug and kiss. Respect their wishes as you show affection, but don't neglect it.

- *Apologize.* No parent is perfect, of course, and our boys need to understand that. When we snap and answer rudely or sarcastically to them or others, we must model apology. It's hard to do but so valuable in the long run. Do you want your son to be the kind of man who never sees and acknowledges his own shortcomings or who is too prideful to ask someone to forgive him? Of course not. So show him how you swallow your pride and admit you're wrong. He'll respect you all the more for it.

My boys would often argue about which book or movie or car was "better." These disagreements could naturally lead to a discussion about differences of opinion. Tell your sons, "Just because you like that game more doesn't mean it's better; it means you prefer it and it's your opinion that the game is better." That important lesson is amplified as they meet others whose lives, beliefs, and cultures are different from theirs. If they've learned respect, they can address those differences respectfully, agreeing to disagree.

Boys don't catch respect simply through osmosis, so we also need to engage in direct instruction about respectful behavior. But saying, "Be kind even if others aren't kind to you" doesn't have as much impact as delivering cookies to that unsmiling neighbor, and being rewarded by a big grin. Here are a few ideas for activities that nurture respect:

- *Create relationships for your boys.* Getting them involved in a sports team or a club often puts them with people who are different from them. They quickly discover that even those who are different have worth, and being part of a team simply reinforces the concept of respect.
- *Volunteer with your children.* Let them see the value of those who live in a different place or within a different social status. Some friends of mine take their children on one mission trip each summer. Their sons have been exposed to homeless people in urban areas and rural Haitian families, and through that their understanding of respect for others has been strengthened.

- *Foster relationships across the ages.* If grandparents aren't close, find a neighbor to adopt. If your sons see the elderly up close and participate in their lives, they'll come away with a stronger sense of respect for others.

As your children are exposed to those who are different culturally or generationally, teach them to talk with people, not at them. Their conversations shouldn't be all about themselves, a litany of their day and adventures. Instead, teach them to ask about others and listen, truly engaging others in conversation.

Growing Respect, from Infant to Teen

Our teaching of respect changes as our children grow. We hope, of course, that they've "caught" it by their elementary years, so at that point all we're doing is reinforcing respect. A look at how respect affects your children at different ages can be helpful.

- Infants are obviously too young to show respect, but they quickly learn to trust those who take care of them. As they get older, it's easier for them to respect those who've laid a foundation of trust.
- Toddlers are learning how to talk and interact with others, so this is a perfect time to teach the importance of saying "please" and "thank you." As they learn to share, they're learning an element of respect for others. As we teach them to put things in their proper places, they learn respect for possessions, as well.
- Preschoolers, especially if they're enrolled in preschool, are learning not only about rules, but about the results of not respecting authority. Reinforcing family rules and consequences at home will strengthen lessons on respect.
- Elementary-aged children are living by rules in the classroom. Many schools have undertaken character education that addresses respect, but Mom can't leave it all up to the

school. If respect has been taught at home in your boys' early years, the classroom will be a time of reinforcement. Elementary-aged boys have a strong sense of what's "right" and "fair." It's hard to be respectful when things don't seem fair, but that's a lesson in itself for this age group.

- Middle schoolers need more freedom than their elementary brothers, but they also need boundaries that show you value them. Peer pressure intervenes in a big way in this age group, and can crowd out respect for others who are different. Reinforcing the importance of your son's being his own boy, and your providing a safe haven at home can help counteract peer pressure and reinforce the importance of respect.

- High school boys need even more independence. Show you respect them by allowing them to make as many choices as you can and giving them some responsibility. When you hand a responsibility to your teenaged son, you're saying, "I trust you to follow through with this." The need for respect within the family grows in this age bracket as the typical teen angst sets in. Even with their down days and blue moods, teen boys need to show respect for others in the family.

In *The Purpose of Boys*, Michael Gurian writes that parents can show they respect their sons by regularly asking questions that help boys see their purpose and intrinsic worth. Boys' answers to the questions below will differ across the ages, but they'll appreciate the respect you show as you encourage them to reflect on who they are and who they can be.

- What is the most important thing you did today?
- What will be the most important thing you do when you're a man?
- Who are your heroes? Why?

The mind of a boy loves to be challenged by important questions. Gurian makes the point that your son stores up those sessions of questioning and teaching for later. Those deposits of time and discussion the first ten years of his life will pay off in the second ten years as he faces the excitement and confusion of adolescence. The question-and-answer sessions pay not only dividends of mother-son trust but bonuses of self-respect, too.[1]

Following the Code: Manners

Manners are a code of conduct that, when used, shows respect to others. Manners are, in fact, an extension of respectful behavior. The behavior of a well-mannered boy says, "I know it's not all about me. There are people at this table who don't want to see me chew with my mouth open, and I respect that." Using manners acknowledges the value of those around us. We're reminded in Philippians 2:3 that our minds are to be set toward others: "Do nothing from selfishness or empty conceit, but with humility of mind regard one another as more important than yourselves" (NASB).

In *Raising a Modern-Day Knight: A Father's Role in Guiding His Son to Authentic Manhood*, Robert Lewis writes of the code of conduct of the medieval knight.[2] As you read the requirements of a knight, consider how these actions show respect for others:

- He was expected to be loyal—to live up to his pledged word. *When a boy shows loyalty, he puts another's needs and desires ahead of his own.*
- He was challenged to conduct himself like a champion in all things, displaying courage and valor. *A boy who shows courage on behalf of others honors them.*
- He was expected to win the esteem of women—to be chivalrous. *A chivalrous boy is polite, courteous, gallant, and mannerly—bound to win a woman's heart!*

- He was required to show largesse or exude generosity. *A generous boy puts his desires on the back burner, and gives willingly to others.*

Boys well understand the concept of honor—they love stories of knights, castles, and jousts. Explaining manners to your son as being like honor to medieval knights may make manners sound more appealing. So use the concept of honor to help reinforce manners. A well-mannered boy is showing honor to those around him just as a knight showed honor to the court.

It's important that boys not see manners as something just *Mom* wants them to do. The parents' united front is important, so the teaching and reinforcement of manners should come from both Mom and Dad. Dad's modeling of manners makes all the difference in the world to a son. Speaking realistically, in a household of five males and one female, there were a few times that I stood up and said, "If that happens one more time at this dinner table, boys, you're on your own. I will not sit here and listen to that. And you can clean up as well." A few times, Dad was included in the "boys," and this was one of those times. But Dad quickly rose to the occasion with, "Boys, that's enough. We all know better," and we were able to finish our dinner as a family.

Here are a few ways to ensure your sons "get" manners:

- *Prepare them.* If you're on your way to a party or some-one's house, tell them what to do if Grandmother serves broccoli, which they can't stand. If you know someone in attendance speaks in an accent that is hard to understand, let your sons know ahead of time. Think ahead and pre-pare your sons for whatever you can.
- *Remind them.* When you drop your sons off at a birthday party, remind them to thank the host or hostess before they come home. Prior to their own birthday celebration,

remind them of what to say when they open a gift they've already received.

- *Compliment them.* When they do remember, tell them that you noticed. Wait until you're in the car, but say something specific, "Grandmother really appreciated your hug and 'thank you' for her gift, Tim. That was great."
- *Make allowances for age.* Obviously your toddler won't be as accomplished at manners as his older brother, but the positive side is that he'll be eager to model his older brother's behavior. Don't snicker at his attempts—and don't let your sons do so—but praise him.
- *Practice.* Most of us with a houseful of boys don't get much opportunity to exercise etiquette, but you can create your own events. I wish I'd taken the time to do this as my boys grew up. The china and good silver sits in that china cabinet, and I could have been using it once a month to set a mock formal dinner for the boys. It would have been a great chance to practice manners. Even in a fast-food restaurant, though, you can practice things like, "Don't begin eating until everyone has been served."

Training in the Essentials

Any child needs to know certain essentials: saying please and thank you, answering the phone correctly, and using good table manners. Again, our boys will model what they see and hear, so it's up to us to be good examples. When it's time for my high school son to take the trash out, I say *please.* When he's done it, I thank him. Yes, it's his job and I do expect him to do it, but I'm thankful that he did, and I show respect by telling him so. Turnabout is fair play because the other night he said to me, "Thanks for doing my laundry, Mom."

Society is more casual today than it was when we were children, but once you and Dad have decided how you want the telephone answered, let the boys practice. Keep paper and pen handy and teach your boys how to ask if someone would like to leave a message. When they need information from a store or the library, let them make the call. Talk them through it first, and make sure they know how to get to the right person.

Table manners will vary according to the location and situation, but decide first on what you expect around your own dinner table. Let the boys know what is expected and what is not tolerated. Be on the same page with your husband, and hold your sons accountable. A friend warned her son that he would eat alone next meal if a certain behavior occurred again. It did, and she called him early for the next meal. He was shocked to find the table set for one, but that was the last time he demonstrated that behavior at the dinner table.

Opening Doors and Other Niceties

Today's casual society is no reason to neglect teaching young men how to act respectfully. My husband opened the door for a woman the other day and she took affront. What to do in that situation? Instead of berating the woman for her difference of opinion, he just smiled and nodded respectfully and went on his way. Our boys will likely encounter the same behavior from women who don't hold the same standards for manners. Teach your sons how to handle it if their genteel display of manners is spurned.

Basically, boys should open a door for a woman and let a woman go first. Depending on the social situation—not in the school cafeteria, for instance—he should stand when a woman enters the room, pull a woman's chair out for her, and offer to walk her to the curb, her car, or her door. If your son has learned to say please and thank you at home, he'll know to employ that liberally in social and dating situations, especially with his date's parents. Earlier lessons about conversing (like "Listen, don't just talk about yourself") will come in handy as well. When my friend's son and his girlfriend broke up, the girl's mother told my friend, "I loved Brian. He was the most polite boy she had ever dated." Good manners go a long way toward endearing a boy to the parents of a date. Check the resource list in appendix B for several great books on manners for growing young men.

It won't be a stretch for your son to treat a girl like a lady if he has grown up in an atmosphere that extends and reinforces respect. Dad's modeling can't be discounted, and if Dad needs a refresher course as you enter a social situation—like a formal dinner or a wedding reception—just gather all the boys for that. Remind Dad that the eyes of small males will be on him that day, and he needs to model great manners for his sons.

Encouraging Healthy Relationships

Attitudes about dating differ among families, but it's safe to say that dating should not be your son's top priority, even during the high school years. It's much healthier to provide group situations for boys and girls than to begin pairing them off. If you desire that your son go to college, or begin a trade, or establish himself before taking on a family, why would you emphasize dating since that may lead him to shortcut his life plan? Perhaps there are situations when the Lord puts couples together early and plants the desire for marriage, but a rational look bears out that married life is much easier when each mate has a well-established personal foundation.

Teenage dating is healthiest when it's approached as a part of life, not the reason for life. The "I have to have a boyfriend" syndrome is probably more prevalent than "I have to have a girlfriend," but guard against that by maintaining a balanced approach to dating. Give your son every opportunity to get together with groups of both sexes in safe environments. Encourage him to have friendships with boys and girls. We all know how important the traits of friendship are to a marriage, so those boy-girl friendships, in balance, can be stepping stones to later, more mature commitment.

Preparing to Be Mother-of-the-Groom

Including this section in the chapter on respect makes sense because that's what you have to have as mother-of-the-groom—respect for your son and his fiancée. When he comes home and announces he's found the one, get to know her! Don't try to be her best friend or crowd your way into the relationship, but let her know you care about her. Your son will appreciate that, as long as you let your daughter-in-law-to-be set the stage for how close your relationship should be. I sent a birthday card to my future daughter-in-law and sent a Christmas card to her family. She came to visit several times, and we got to know each other. We e-mailed each other on occasion before their marriage and we do so now. (But now that they're married, I get to buy presents like earrings and cute tops and pink stationery. We finally got our girl!) Stay open, though, to your son's feelings about his intended. Don't take over and don't crowd—even though the thought of adding a girl to the family is wonderful!

Remember that even though you may have wanted to plan a wedding ever since you planned your own, this one is *not* yours to plan. A mother of the groom does have a few specific duties, but beyond those, it's up to the bride and groom to decide if they need your help on anything else. Here are some of those duties:

- Make contact with the bride's parents, if you haven't already. We'd gotten to know each other a bit through e-mail, so it wasn't awkward to begin e-mailing each other to coordinate wedding plans.
- Attend whatever showers you can. Our families were separated geographically, and we wanted everyone here to meet our son's bride, so some friends hosted a shower for her here before the wedding.
- Choose your dress after the bride's mother chooses hers. Follow her lead on formality—long or short dress, kinds of accessories, and so forth. You're not obligated to match

anyone, and the old adage, "Wear beige and keep your mouth shut" is still circulating. Getting just the right dress was difficult for me. I didn't want to look too matronly or too hip, so I had to search for a while. As it turned out, I found a great beige dress!

- Provide a guest list for your side of the family. Be sure to give accurate names and addresses, and mark any eccentricities of people on the list (like "Don't seat Uncle Jim by Aunt Sally").
- Plan and host the rehearsal dinner. This is the fun part! This is your reception, so have a good time with it. We surprised the groom with a video of his growing up years. There was a lot of laughter and, at the end, there wasn't a dry eye in the house.
- Offer to help with anything the bride and groom need. As it turned out, we had some things that could be used for the reception to save the bride and groom some money, so we were able to help in that way.

Believe it or not, there are several books about being mother-of-the-groom (see appendix B). The most important thing is to be sensitive to the couple's needs and not encroach on the planning of what is, indeed, their day.

Respect Is Reciprocal

My mother always told me, "You get back what you've given out." I've found that to be true as a mom and as a teacher. If you show respect to others—your sons, your daughter-in-law-to-be, or your mate—you're more likely to be paid in kind. Respect is the basis for effective manners, healthy dating relationships, and healthy family relationships, so make it a priority with your sons.

9

A Band of Brothers

Then Joseph said to his brothers, "Come close to me."
GENESIS 45:4

The story of Joseph and his brothers is classic. Twelve boys, but their father, Jacob, favors Joseph above the others. Genesis 37:4 tells us, "When his brothers saw that their father loved him more than any of them, they hated him and could not speak a kind word to him." The boys conspire to sell Joseph to slave traders and fake his death to conceal their deed from their father. Joseph endures hard labor and imprisonment, but is finally elevated to a position in the royal household. When he encounters his brothers once again, they are in need because of a famine. God allows Joseph to see that what they meant for evil, God meant for good. Armed with this understanding, Joseph extends a hand to his brothers, just as God did for him, and he is able to draw his brothers close. You can read the entire story in Genesis chapters 37–50.

The application for today's boy mom? Consider Joseph's words to his brothers: "You intended to harm me, but God intended it for good, to accomplish ... the saving of many lives" (Gen. 50:20). No matter where you are on the parenting marathon or what has gone on before, God is able to take it all and use it for good in the lives of your boys. We won't always be here to maintain harmony and patch things up between our sons, but we can help them learn how to take that responsibility on themselves. We can enable them to be a band of brothers not easily broken.

In today's society, more than ever before, our sons may need that brother bond. Recent studies by Duke University and the University of Arizona indicate that Americans have experienced a shrinking in their circle of close and trusted friends. The number of adults who feel they have no sounding board with whom to discuss personal and important issues has doubled in the last nineteen years. Participants in this study showed, however, a much smaller loss in family connections. Lynn Smith-Lovin, one of the study's authors said, "The evidence shows that Americans have fewer confidants, and those ties are also more family-based than they used to be."[1] The amount of time spent at work and the influence of virtual Internet communities may be two of the causes of this reduction in real-life social ties. With fewer confidants outside the family, our sons will need each other even more.

When the Family Dynamic Changes...

In science, the study of dynamics examines forces and how they relate to motion and equilibrium. When we look at family dynamics, we see that each of our sons has an effect on the family unit, and together the family finds a balance, a harmony. Add or remove a son from that equation, and the family unit has to reorient itself.

Families are not so surprised by change when a new son enters the picture. It's a time of change for everyone, and if the other boys are still small they're still growing and changing. But once the family has hit a plateau of sorts with sons developing into older children and teens, a change in the family dynamic can take us off guard.

Our four sons are each three years apart, almost to the month. Even though they were evenly spaced, their dad and I always referred to the older two as "the big ones" and the younger two as "the little ones." That made a tidy package: "You take the little ones to the restroom and I'll wait in line with the big ones." But when the "biggest one" left for college, the family dynamic shifted. I was surprised to learn that the boys would relate to one another differently each time a brother left the day-to-day picture.

We don't always like to hear that change is unavoidable, but it's true. Change in the relationships between your sons is inevitable. It's understandable that sibling closeness may decline in early adulthood with the pressures of marriage, new family, job, and so on, but it often rises again in later years. So while their preoccupation with their own lives is a factor in brothers' changing relationships, there are other factors as well.

When One Moves Out...

As your sons leave the nest, their differences become more apparent. They're out choosing their own roads now, figuring out who they have the potential to be, and exercising their unique skills and abilities to their fullest extent. Some young men exercise that freedom by choosing different ideological roads than their siblings, and this can be a point of contention. ("Dude— you've changed! Where's the guy that was so totally against that in high school!" or "Hey, Bro, you're just holding onto whatever you've always been taught, never questioning anything.")

Geography is a factor, too. Yes, today we have many ways to connect technologically, but nothing takes the place of the entire family gathered in one kitchen for a family birthday. Long-distance brothers can remain close, but it takes some effort; it doesn't just happen. Moms can help both now and later to maintain their sons' brotherly bonds amidst a sea of change.

It's hard to predict exactly how one son's move will affect your boys, but the more you involve them and prepare them, the easier it will be. If you concentrate on the son leaving and ignore his siblings, you'll likely experience a bigger hole when the leaving son departs. First, acknowledge that life is about to change for everyone. Here are some tips to help with that adjustment:

- *Involve your boys in the process.* Don't be afraid to talk about it. As you shop for the son who's moving out, take a brother or two along. Let him pick out something for the brother's new apartment or dorm room. Let the brothers who will remain at home be a part of this exciting time.

- *Encourage normalcy.* Encourage your sons to be happy for the brother who is branching out. Let them see this as a normal, exciting part of life that they can look forward to.
- *Plan visits.* Talk about Thanksgiving and Christmas when Big Brother will be home, but try to plan a family visit to the campus, too. And if your next son is old enough, a visit on his own to see his college brother is always a great treat.
- *Prepare for his first trip back home.* That first return visit home is difficult as a son tries to balance family and old friends. Remind the sons who are still at home that your eldest won't be available all the time, and if it's Thanksgiving, this is a short visit. They have to share Big Brother, but there will be more time later.
- *Reapportion family responsibilities.* If the eldest always mowed the lawn, this will fall to another son, but remember to move other duties down to the younger ones as well. Be sensitive and don't load everything on one brother.
- *Help your boys step up to their new places.* In a family of boys, the second in command will now see himself as top dog. Help him with that new responsibility. He needs to learn to use it wisely and not to abuse it.
- *Institute a new family holiday—Brother's Day.* We celebrate Mother's Day and Father's Day, but not a day for siblings. As a family, choose a day (maybe before the first son takes off) and have the boys celebrate that together. They can continue the tradition for years to come.
- *Maintain contact.* Use technology to help the boys keep in touch. Cell phones, texting, and e-mail are great for this, as your boys can make quick contact with one another. If the ones at home are too young or you've chosen not to go the personal cell phone route, remind your college son to call perhaps once a week. Always make time for him to talk with his brothers as well as you and Dad. Ask him the

best times for his brothers to call him, so they'll all be more likely to have time to talk. When you send a package to the son who's away, let the brothers include a note or pick out a special treat to enclose. This will help both the son who's away and the ones who remain at home feel closer.

In the boys-plus household, when one moves out, the dynamics can change a bit more drastically. Mom, if your firstborn is a daughter or was born between the boys, you'll see a definite shift in your household when she leaves the nest. Your pink anchor is gone, and now you're adrift in a sea of guys.

Since firstborns are usually leaders, if your firstborn is a daughter and she leaves the nest, encourage the next boy in line to step up. Let him see how this gives him the opportunity to develop leadership skills and help guide his brothers.

If your daughter is in the middle, her absence may allow the next-older son and the next-younger son to see a new opportunity to connect. I have a friend whose middle child is a daughter, and she left for college just as the eldest son graduated and came home to live and work. The seven-year span between her eldest and youngest son had loomed large before, but now that they're fifteen and twenty-two, they relate more easily. They're having a great time, hanging out together as "the boys." But the household has definitely shifted toward the male perspective, as Mom finds herself the only woman in the house.

The bottom line is, be flexible. Realize that relationships will grow and change as the siblings do the same. Be there now to guide them through those dynamics so they can learn to maneuver through them later on their own.

When the Brother Bond Is Tested...

The last thing you want is for your growing sons to engage in the same old sibling rivalry that may have plagued their childhood. How to prevent that? Avoid the same things now that you tried to avoid when they were children: favoritism and labeling. Our attempts to be fair should continue even as our sons grow. This is easy when they're all making choices we approve of, but when one chooses an unexpected path, we need to keep our love stable and constant, evenly applied. The words of Psalm 139:14 echo in our hearts as we remember that our sons are "fearfully and wonderfully made," evidence that God's "works are wonderful." We need to let go of those labels we may have bought into when they were little: "This is the smart one," or "He'll be the starving artist." If we label our sons, they all too often grow into those labels, and they stop there. This leaves them with no chance to branch out, to break out, and to become who they really are gifted to be. So leave favoritism and labeling behind, if you haven't already.

As your boys leave the nest, those brotherly ties stretch and sometimes they even snap. One son may call you and say, "Jim is drivin' me crazy! When we talk, all he does is put down what I'm doing and talk about his great ventures." Or you may not sense a problem until you all get together, and you can cut the tension with a knife. Granted, as young men, they need to work out their problems themselves, but sometimes they need a little coaching to learn just how to approach that. Here are a few things you can tell your older sons that may help them in dealing with one another:

- *Don't compare*—jobs, goals, girlfriends, spouses, choice of car, location, and so forth. Focus on your own goals and don't hold them up to your brother's. Insist that your brother do the same.
- *Don't "bait" and don't respond to "baiting."* You know each other's "hot buttons" and sometimes like to push one just to get a rise out of your brother. Rise above that—leave baiting behind, and don't sink to that level if you're being baited.
- *Be willing to say "I'm sorry" and "I forgive you"*—both of you. Don't always be the one to wait for an apology. Remember,

sometimes you're wrong, too. Remember that 2 Corinthians 2:7–8 says that when a brother errs, we "ought to forgive and comfort him, so he will not be overwhelmed by excessive sorrow.... Reaffirm your love for him."

- *Don't be sarcastic*—especially when you text or e-mail. Sarcasm isn't always interpreted the way it's meant, and that is especially true when you're not face-to-face. One cannot interpret the tone in the printed word, so sarcasm can easily be misinterpreted in e-mail and texting.
- *Don't respond when you're angry.* If your conversation becomes tense and heated, walk away for a minute. Proverbs 21:23 teaches, "He who guards his mouth and his tongue keeps himself from calamity." Take a minute to cool off and pick up your conversation later so you won't say something you regret.
- *Don't just talk, listen.* And be honest with one another. If there's a problem, don't let it fester, but bring it up and discuss it.
- *Make contact with your brothers*—don't let them do all the calling. Remember the words of Romans 12:10: "Be devoted to one another in brotherly love. Honor one another above yourselves."
- *Make time for your brothers*—but realize that they have lives, too. Don't infringe on their lives or monopolize them.

Why am I telling you this, Mom? Because the day may come when your son will call you and say, "I just can't talk to my brother anymore!" Pull out a couple of these ideas and see if you can help your sons through the conflict. But remember it is ultimately their job to resolve their own conflicts. I remember saying to one son, "I understand, but the things you're saying to me you need to be saying to your brother. Call him, talk to him, and tell him why you feel this way." They have, and they've learned—and they continue to learn.

As Their Needs Change...

Not only does the relationship between the brothers change, but their need for you changes, just as it did as they were growing up. The calls will come more frequently for Dad, as boys maintain their own cars, contemplate major purchases, and file income tax. Remember chapter 1? When they were babies, they were just little bundles of childhood, but now they're indisputably male, and the camaraderie with Dad is strong. But Mom, they still need your love and your prayers and, once in a while, your guidance.

You can help them through relationship changes by just being there for them whenever they need you. You can help them remember each other's birthdays and anniversaries—a simple text is a great reminder. Get them all together whenever you can, and if one isn't able to come, call him and pass around the phone or use the webcam. Allow for differences in their personalities, locations, and occupations, and, Mom, love them unconditionally. That way, you'll support them through the changes in their lives and help them remain brothers of the heart.

10

A Word from the Boys

Now you, brothers, like Isaac, are children of promise.

GALATIANS 4:28

Now we hear from the boys themselves. You'll get a glimpse into their "boydom" and find out what they think worked, what was great, what was hard. You'll hear about the brother bond in their own words. Hearing from the boys themselves may help you see the experience of growing up in a home of boys from their perspective.

What was great about growing up with brothers?

It appears that giving boys space just to be boys is a good thing. Imagination, creativity, and activity seem to be keys to a happy boyhood. When asked what was great about growing up with three brothers, Benjamin, the youngest said, "It was fun! There was always something to do or something going on."

Andrew, the third son, answered, "Where can I begin? Cops and robbers, wrestling in the yard, riding bikes, trips to the park, selling lemonade … the list is endless."

Matthew, our second son, combined adventure with creativity and used the built-in cast of brothers: "I'd come up with short stories and plays, and I did a number of videos, casting my brothers in my films. Having three brothers made for entertaining vacations; what would be fun with a small family was even more fun with three brothers."

Jonathan, the oldest, summed it up this way: "I always had three boys to adventure with. Spending time with the brothers, I traveled back to the Old West as a cowboy, chased down criminals as a police officer, battled raging infernos as a fireman, and fought wars as a soldier."

What was hard about growing up with brothers?

Even though the boys sent me their answers individually and didn't collaborate, it's interesting that they seemed to agree on the difficulties of a houseful of brothers. Jonathan said, "In any house with as many as four children, there's a great deal of jockeying for position. As the oldest, I was naturally the leader, but I had no qualms about forcing my status on my brothers when I shouldn't have. I'm sure this was hard on my brothers, and it was something that invariably led to conflict." And what does the youngest say? "I was always getting muscled out, but no hard feelings ..."

Andrew cut right to the heart of the matter as he wrote, "Two words: sibling rivalry. Every brother wants to be the top dog, and if your house is occupied by more than one child, that is mathematically impossible. But that never stopped any of us from trying to establish dominance. Sometimes this led to arguments, fights, and some wounded egos." Matthew wrote about how all the testosterone in the household sometimes led to a snowball effect. "Four different brothers, four different opinions—and we all had to weigh in, even if it started as a conflict between only two. But we learned to work it out."

What highlights of family life stand out?

Family vacations took first place as a big hit. Since I'm a teacher and my husband does freelance work, we're able to take off for a couple of weeks in the summer. We'd pack all four boys, and sometimes the dog, into the van and venture out, armed with an itinerary and lots of juice boxes. One summer we visited Yellowstone National Park. It was a long drive from Florida, but the good times and accumulated memories were worth the trip. We all rode horses, the boys hiked to the top of a "mountain" outside the lodge, and we explored all the natural wonders the park had to offer.

Benjamin couldn't nail down one best memory but said, "Some of the most fun and favorite family times I can remember with my brothers have to be our yearly summer vacation trips. I do have to say my favorite vacation was when we visited Yellowstone National Park and stayed at the lodge in the woods."

Jonathan expanded on the value of family vacations: "As a kid, I traveled all over the country, seeing places that I otherwise would probably never have seen, and sharing experiences that deepened the bond of our family relationships. Sometimes it felt like the van just wasn't big enough for the six of us (plus the dog!), but I attribute much of our current closeness to the long days and nights we spent on the road."

Andrew also recalled "surprises" as a highlight, which were part of the family vacation. I had a "Surprise Bag" that contained a big plastic bag for each son. Inside were small toys, games, or books to keep them occupied. They had each packed their own backpacks with things to entertain them on the trip, but these surprises were inexpensive things to relieve boredom. There was usually a midmorning and a midafternoon surprise as we often drove from early morning until bedtime. Sometimes a more expensive surprise would be given with the news that this was a "two-in-one." Mom and Dad could always count on a little peace and quiet for a while after surprises were doled out.

Andrew wrote, "Surprises worked! I can see now that it was a clever scheme to keep us occupied rather than bothering Mom and Dad, but boy, were they great! The anticipation began building once we left the hotel. As it got closer to lunch time, the ever-present question moved from our little minds to our little mouths: 'Is it time for surprises?'"

In writing about the highlights of daily family life, Jonathan confirms that what parents do and say each day does matter. Kids see it all. "What sticks out to me was the life I saw lived out each day by my parents. We had theological discussions over Sunday lunch, and talked through what we were learning. But my parents integrated their faith into their everyday lives: the resolution of difficulty in my family was marked with prayer, and I distinctly remember my parents apologizing to me more than once for losing their tempers. My parents didn't just talk about their faith, they lived it to us, and their example has a great deal to do with who we are today."

How do you feel about limits on technology?

It seems the boys feel that Mom's attitude toward technology was right in the long run. One rule the boys didn't mention was that if anyone's homework required the computer, that had priority over computer play time. So brothers had to wait until all computer homework was done to begin playing. Computer rules were posted, and the order went by age. If the oldest took the last turn, the second oldest got the first turn the next day. Once, when one of the boys had a friend over who was an only child, they quickly noticed his dismay at having to wait for three others to take their turns! We talked about it later, and they came to the conclusion that an only child's unlimited computer time might be great, but they'd rather have brothers!

Jonathan rather bluntly wrote, "As kids, we were basically forced outside. We didn't have game systems or cable, and our turns on the computer were limited to thirty minutes each. So we had lots of down time, and Mom was constantly encouraging us to go outside. We fished, rode our bikes, tried unsuccessfully to master tennis and racquetball, built numerous forts out of scrap wood, climbed trees, played street hockey—I could go on and on. But it was healthy for us. Instead of zoning out in front of the television for hours before dinner, we got plenty of exercise growing up and had experiences that broadened our horizons."

Benjamin, short and sweet and always right to the point, said, "Although we always wanted more computer turns, the time limits did seem to work. Everyone got a chance, and it was a smart choice because it forced us to seek other ways of using our imagination." Andrew felt that taking turns at the computer as well as taking turns getting the front seat of the van worked because "both of these strategies taught us that we were all equals. No brother was better than another; none of us deserved more benefits than the other. In a family, there's giving and taking. We're sensitive to each other's needs, and no matter what happens, we continue to love each other. These strategies put those principles into practice."

I asked the boys what they intend to do if they have a houseful of boys. The youngest said it was just too weird to think that far ahead. It's not so far ahead for Jonathan, though, and he wrote, "I will let them be boys. Keep them out of the house and off the computer and video games. I would have wasted my childhood in front of a screen if our time had not been limited. Catching tadpoles, jumping bike ramps, and building tree forts didn't just entertain me; it taught me, and it will teach my boys as well."

Can you be "your own boy" among a bunch of brothers?

It's interesting to note the value the boys put on being your own person. Matthew, who just graduated from college with a film degree, feels that this is one of the things many parents neglect. When thinking about their child's future, they're thinking only in terms of stability or security, and "security is one thing that is not always guaranteed when you devote your life to anything in the creative arts because there's a substantial risk in order to achieve the reward." He goes on to write, "My parents gave me latitude and had the patience for me to reach my goal to be in the film industry. Ever since I was young, my mother with her background in English and drama strongly influenced my love of story and how art can convey a variety of things."

Oh, the Sunday afternoon plays and the rainy day videos—all the brothers were involved in them to some extent. Matthew writes, "This had varying results and we were not without conflict, but it did over time build a strong passion to create and produce my creative stories." Matthew feels that three specific things helped him with his dream. He writes, "My parents would constantly encourage me and help me out when I was in a jam. Second, they would express their opinions and give advice, but they kept a healthy distance for me to grow myself. And last, once I reached a certain age, they helped surround me with the proper tools I needed to be able to explore film, whether that was trips to the library to check out multiple films, going to the multiplex, or sending me across the country to Los Angeles for film school."

Matthew feels that one problem with youth today is not that they don't have the ability to do great and creative things, but "that they grow up in environments where that is not much of an option, so they don't develop that passion over time." He thinks we parents should "allow children to follow their dreams and shoot for the stars."

On the subject of being one's own boy, Andrew writes that when he's a parent, he will "make sure every boy has the chance to do what he wants to do. My wife and I will try to encourage each boy's talents and abilities and make sure to affirm them. Boys need to be affirmed and told that they are valuable and that what they do matters."

A balance of independence and guidance isn't easy to achieve, and working alongside your boys may not instill in them the desire to follow you into your line of business. It's effective, though, in strengthening bonds and instilling an understanding of family as a team.

Jonathan writes, "Our parents involved us in the things they loved. I got my love of English from my mom and my mechanical aptitude from working on the car with my father. Mom took us to the library in the summer, and during that time I read every Hardy Boys mystery and Sherlock Holmes story I could get my hands on. Just the other day, Dad and I made plans to change the wheel bearings in my car together later this summer. To this day, one of the ways I bond with Dad best is to work on a project with him."

Can brothers also be friends?

They're young men now, but the brother bond is still there, and I pray it will stay strong over the years. Andrew writes, "The best thing about growing up in a house of boys was having three best friends. They say there's 'a friend that sticks closer than a brother,' but I've had the best of both worlds; I had three brothers who are friends. I can't imagine what growing up would have been like without them. My brothers are part of who I am and who I will become. I've laughed with them and cried with them, and I wouldn't trade those experiences for anything."

The viewpoint of the youngest brother is different in some ways, but Benjamin, who still lives at home, shares his impression of the brother bond as he writes, "Not having your brothers around gives you a different viewpoint. There are upsides (like computer time and use of the car), but I do miss them, which is a downside. But we're brothers. We keep in touch. We call, we text, and we do get to see each other during the summer and holidays."

Matthew and Jonathan both expressed how the brother bond is closer than friendship. Matthew writes, "I had relationships with friends who disappointed me in middle school, but my brothers were always there for me." Jonathan expands as he writes, "I had a few friends who were the only child, and when I spent time with them, I realized what a blessing my brothers were. I think my brothers are part of the reason I have such high expectations today for friendships. As a boy, I had three best friends. I doubt if there are many people who could say they had one friend like that, but I had (and still have) three. My brothers' love and friendship never flinched, no matter what. They were always there for me as my best friends, not because it made them more or less popular, but because we were brothers and that's what brothers do."

A Final Word from Mom

Boys are bundles of promise. Future fathers, husbands, teachers, pastors, filmmakers…and who knows what else? Mother of sons, what a blessing you've been given. Handle it with care, being "joyful in hope, patient in affliction, faithful in prayer" (Rom. 12:12).

Appendix A

Dad's Part in All of This

Then our sons in their youth will be like well-
nurtured plants.

PSALM 144:12

This book is not an attempt to discount the role of the father in raising boys. Rather, its goal is to help mothers who are the minority in their households understand their role in mothering their sons. A shared burden is lessened, and both moms and sons need a dad's help. Both parents need to be on the same page in the parenting plan, and that takes communication.

Talk with your husband about what you both want as goals in raising your sons. Share with each other experiences from your own childhoods and reap both the good and the bad from those experiences. Learn lessons from where you've been and what you've experienced. Mom, communicate your needs and fears about mothering boys with your husband. Tell him what's going on between you and the boys. Let him rejoice in the good, and help you with the bad.

If the two of you are not already a team, become one. Not just a husband and wife team, but a parenting team with common goals. Put yourselves on the same page. Share the following pages with your husband so he can see what's critical in raising sons who are physically, mentally, and spiritually healthy, and how the two of you can accomplish that. Let him read, and then talk together. Be intentional. Plan together.

Embark on the parenting marathon together. Grab one another by the hand, and run side by side. The route is scary, hilarious, and breathtaking. Take it all in, with parallel hearts.

FOR DAD...

Chapter 1—Great Expectations

Your wife is now contending with an alien form—boys. Many women have no frame of reference for those blue bundles of energy. What can you do?

- Help her to understand boys. You remember more than she'll ever know about the species.
- Indulge her in pink once in a while. When the majority in your household is male, femininity seems alien. Bring her flowers; buy her something pink.
- Go see a chick flick with her once in a while, even if you're not that interested.
- Encourage her to maintain close friendships with other women. Parent the boys alone while she goes to Bible study or a ladies prayer group.

Chapter 2—The Magnet Syndrome (aka Sibling Rivalry)

This chapter is all about sibling rivalry. "Boys will be boys" goes only so far, and it's probably best for you not to repeat that adage. Help your wife understand boys' desires for dominance, and together come up with a plan to channel that.

- Don't show favoritism among the boys, as that just fuels sibling rivalry.
- Don't let the boys hurt each other—verbally or physically.
- Give each son a chance to be a leader at something.

Chapter 3—Intentional Parenting

You have to be intentional about parenting; you have to parent on purpose. This takes real teamwork between Mom and Dad.

- Make every effort to know each boy's strengths and weaknesses, and foster the uniqueness of each son.
- Decide together how you will parent each son
    physically.
    intellectually.
    socially.
    spiritually.
- Don't let parenting just happen; plan for it. Consult the recommended reading list in appendix B for helps.

Chapter 4—The Education of Boys

Boys and school sometimes don't mix well. Together, you and your wife can smooth that road for your sons.

- Get involved in their education, teaching them from toddlerhood about all they see around them. Foster a love of learning.
- Visit your sons' school(s). Dads don't often do that, so you'll make a big splash! Have lunch with your son or bring cupcakes on his birthday.

Work with your wife to awaken your sons' natural curiosity through family discussions about the news, current events, history, your work, and your passion.

Chapter 5—Boy Talk

You know firsthand the differences in male-female communication, and you've learned to bridge the gap to some extent with your wife. Now help your sons learn how.

- Talk to your boys before they can even talk.
- Talk to your wife, sharing what you've learned about male-female communication.
- As your boys grow, share with them and model effective and appropriate communication.
- Be home for dinner and help engage the family in dinner-time conversation.

Chapter 6—The Big O's—Order and Organization

Realize that organization teaches discipline, self-control, and personal responsibility. Those are qualities parents hope to instill in their sons, but it doesn't happen by accident. You need a family plan.

- Help Mom with a family powwow to help make organizational decisions.
- If the boys are too young, you and Mom come up with a plan that will work for both of you.
- Don't bail out your sons if they forget or ignore their responsibilities; hold them accountable.
- Provide a file box for each of your sons in their teen years and work with them to organize their lives.

Chapter 7—Media in a Young Man's Life

You're aware of media's allure for the male visual mind. Help your wife capture that power for good and not for ill as you channel your sons' watching habits and teach them to discern.

- Model wise media choices, always aware that little eyes are watching you.
- Work with Mom on a plan for controlling technology in your home.
- Dialogue with your sons about what they see and hear so that they learn to discern for themselves as they grow.

Chapter 8—*Growing Respect*

Respect is a foundation for this chapter, which addresses how to teach your sons to show that they value others. Respect for authority, themselves, and others is examined.

- Model respect for your sons and for your wife. How do you talk about your boss, your pastor, your neighbor, or the guy in the car in front of you?
- Reinforce manners as a way to show honor to others, and strive to be a good example of this.
- Show your sons how to treat a lady as you model respect for their mom. Much of what your boys learn about male-female relationships will come from your example.

Chapter 9—*A Band of Brothers*

The ties that bind your sons to each other will strain and sometimes break as they grow older. Be ready for those changes and for your changing role, as well.

- When it's time for a son to move out, get involved and get your sons involved.
- Take the opportunity to get close to the sons still at home and help them through the changes.
- Help your sons look forward to their own independence.
- Work with your wife through the changing family dynamic.

Chapter 10—A Word from the Boys

There are ups and downs in a houseful of boys. Take the opportunity to share some of your own boyhood with your wife and sons, using those experiences to illustrate lessons for your family.

- Talk about the family dynamics in your boyhood home.
- Share lessons you learned in your boyhood.
- Find a way to highlight each son individually. Help him reach for his dream.
- Assess your family's attitude toward or dependence on technology.
- Talk with your wife and sons about how to create family memories—trips, traditions, and everyday fun.
- Evaluate your own sibling relationships. What has held you together or pushed you apart? How can you use those experiences to help your sons as they grow?

Appendix B

Recommended Reading

General Reading on Raising Sons

Dobson, James C. *Bringing up Boys: Practical Advice and Encouragement for Those Shaping the Next Generation of Men.* Carol Stream, IL: Tyndale, 2005.

Dobson, James C. *The Wonderful World of Boys.* Carol Stream, IL: Tyndale, 2005.

Erwin, Cheryl L. *The Everything Parent's Guide to Raising Boys.* Avon: Adams Media, 2006.

Gurian, Michael. *The Good Son: Shaping the Moral Development of Our Boys and Young Men.* New York: Penguin Putnam, 1999.

Gurian, Michael. *The Purpose of Boys: Helping Our Sons Find Meaning, Significance, and Direction in Their Lives.* Hoboken, NJ: John Wiley & Sons, Inc., 2009.

Meeker, Meg. *Boys Should Be Boys: Seven Secrets to Raising Healthy Sons.* Washington, DC: Regnery, 2008.

Oliver, Gary and Carrie Oliver. *Raising Sons and Loving It: Helping Your Boys Become Godly Men.* Grand Rapids: Zondervan, 2000.

Manners

Bridges, John. *How to Be a Gentleman: A Timely Guide to Timeless Manners*. Nashville: Thomas Nelson, 2008.

Bridges, John and Bryan Curtis. *A Gentleman Gets Dressed Up: What to Wear, When to Wear It, How to Wear It*. Nashville: Thomas Nelson, 2003.

Bridges, John and Bryan Curtis. *As a Gentleman Would Say: Responses to Life's Important (and Sometimes Awkward) Situations*. Nashville: Thomas Nelson, 2001.

Bridges, John and Bryan Curtis. *Fifty Things Every Gentleman Should Know*. Nashville: Thomas Nelson, 2006.

Eberly, Sheryl. *365 Manners Kids Should Know: Games, Activities, and Other Fun Ways to Help Children Learn Etiquette*. New York: Crown Publishing, 2001.

West, Kay. *How to Raise a Gentleman: A Civilized Guide to Helping Your Son Through His Uncivilized Childhood*. Nashville: Thomas Nelson, 2001.

Family Dinners

Doherty, William J. *The Intentional Family: Simple Rituals to Strengthen Family Ties*. Toronto: Addison-Wesley Longman, 1997.

Harris, Samela. *On a Shoestring: Recipes from the House of the Raising Sons*. Australia: Wakefield Press, 1996.

Weinstein, Miriam. *The Surprising Power of Family Meals: How Eating Together Makes Us Smarter, Stronger, Healthier and Happier*. New York: Bantam, 2006.

Reading, Media, and Technology

Baehr, Ted. *The Media-Wise Family: A Family Guide to Making Morally and Spiritually Responsible Decisions about Movies, TV and Multimedia*. St. Louis: Amerisearch, 2005.

Barr, Catherine. *Best New Media, K–12: A Guide to Movies, Subscription Web Sites, and Educational Software and Games*. United States: Libraries Unlimited, Inc., 2008.

Detweiler, Craig. *Into the Dark: Seeing the Sacred in the Top Films of the 21st Century*. Grand Rapids: Baker, 2008.

Dutwin, David. *Unplug Your Kids: A Parent's Guide to Raising Happy, Active, and Well-Adjusted Children in the Digital Age*. Cincinnati: Adams Media Corporation, 2009.

Gurian, Michael. *What Stories Does My Son Need?* New York: Penguin Putnam, 2000.

Hunt, Gladys. *Honey for a Child's Heart: The Imaginative Use of Books in Family Life*. Grand Rapids: Zondervan, 2002.

Hunt, Gladys and Barbara Hampton. *Honey for a Teen's Heart: Using Books to Communicate with Teens*. Grand Rapids: Zondervan, 2002.

Hunt, Gladys and Barbara Hampton. *Read for Your Life: Turning Teens into Readers*. Grand Rapids: Zondervan, 1992.

Odean, Kathleen. *Great Books for Boys*. New York: Ballantine, 1998.

Tobias, Todd, and Lou Harry. *Kid Culture: The Hip Parent's Handbook to Navigating Books, Music, T.V. and Movies in the Digital Age*. Kennebunkport: Cider Mill Press, 2008.

Trelease, Jim. *The Read-Aloud Handbook*. 6th ed. New York: Penguin, 2006.

Wilson, Elizabeth Laraway. *Books Children Love: A Guide to the Best Children's Literature*. Wheaton: Crossway, 2002.

Life Preparation

Harrison, Harry H. *1001 Things Every College Student Needs to Know: Like Buying Your Books Before Exams Start*. Nashville: Thomas Nelson, 2008.

Harrison, Harry H. *1001 Things Every Teen Should Know Before They Leave Home (Or Else They'll Come Back)*. Nashville: Thomas Nelson, 2007.

Harrison, Harry H. *1001 Things Your Kids Should See and Do (Or Else They'll Never Leave Home)*. Nashville: Thomas Nelson, 2007.

General Reading for Single Moms

Chisholm, Dana. *Single Moms Raising Boys*. Kansas City: Beacon Hill, 2006.

Howe, Michele. *Going It Alone: Meeting the Challenges of Being a Single Mom*. Peabody, MA: Hendrickson, 1999.

Howe, Michele. *Pilgrim Prayers for Single Mothers*. Cleveland, OH: The Pilgrim Press, 2002.

Howe, Michele. *Still Going It Alone: Mothering With Faith and Finesse When the Children Have Grown*. Peabody, MA: Hendrickson, 2009.

Howe, Michele. *Successful Single Moms: Thirteen Stories of Triumph*. Cleveland, OH: The Pilgrim Press, 2003.

Osborne, Susan Titus and Lucille Moses. *Rest Stops for Single Mothers: Devotions to Encourage You on Your Journey*. Nashville: B&H, 1985.

Panettieri, Gina and Philip S. Hall. *The Single Mother's Guide to Raising Remarkable Boys*. Cincinnati: Adams Media Corporation, 2008

Reed, Bobbie. *Single Mothers Raising Sons*. Nashville: Thomas Nelson, 1988.

Rodgers, Joan E., Michael F. Cataldo, and William Rodgers. *Raising Sons: Practical Strategies for Single Mothers*. New York: Penguin, 1985.

Thomas, Angela. *My Single Mom Life: Stories and Practical Lessons for Your Journey*. Nashville: Thomas Nelson, 2008.

Turner, Janine. *Holding Her Head High: Twelve Single Mothers Who Championed Their Children and Changed History*. Nashville: Thomas Nelson, 2008.

Especially for Moms

Courtney, Vicki. *Your Boy: Raising a Godly Son in an Ungodly World*. Nashville: B&H, 2006.

Hanson, Mark Victor, LeAnn Thieman, Barbara LoMonaco, and Jack Canfield. *Chicken Soup for the Mother and Son Soul:*

Stories to Celebrate the Lifelong Bond. Deerfield Beach, FL: Health Communications, 2006.

Kingsbury, Karen. *Be Safe Little Boy: Words of Love for Moms*. Grand Rapids: Inspirio, 2006.

Naylor, Sharon. *The Mother of the Groom: Everything You Need to Know to Enjoy the Best Wedding Ever*. New York: Kensington, 2007.

Rabin, Sydell. *The Complete Mother of the Groom: How to Be Graceful, Helpful and Happy During This Special Time*. Cincinnati, OH: Adams Media Corporation, 2009.

Especially for Dads

Bell, James Stuart. *The One Year Men of the Bible: 365 Meditations on Men of Character*. Carol Stream, IL: Tyndale, 2008.

Harrison, Harry H. *Father to Son: Life Lessons on Raising a Boy*. New York: Workman, 2000.

Iggulden, Conn and Hal Iggulden. *The Dangerous Book for Boys*. New York: HarperCollins, 2007.

Lewis, Robert. *Raising a Modern-Day Knight: A Father's Role in Guiding His Son to Authentic Manhood*. Carol Stream, IL: Tyndale, 2007.

Shoemaker, Tim. *Dangerous Devotions for Guys: Dare to Live Your Faith*. Loveland: Group Publishing, 2009.

Appendix C

A Special Word to Single Moms Raising Sons

There's plenty of advice in this book that applies to any mother of sons—married or single. But as a single mother raising sons (widowed, divorced, never married), you find yourself in a unique place, and the hints below are written especially with you in mind.

Take care of yourself—physically, spiritually, emotionally, and socially.

- Stay healthy. You have to be incredibly busy, but don't miss meals, sleep, and regular checkups. You'll model self-respect for your sons in that way.
- Get involved in a community of believers. You need them, your sons need them, your sons need you, and you need the Lord.
- Maintain a personal quiet time of devotional reading and prayer. You need to be recharged each day.

- Find a confidante or mentor. You need a friend to talk to, so ask the Lord to lead you to someone wise.

Accept your sons' differences.

- Acknowledge that they're different from you, and their actions and reactions will not necessarily be what you expect.
- Acknowledge that your sons are different from each other. Nurture their individuality.
- Have fun raising this alien species called "boy"! Be sure to pick up a copy of *The Dangerous Book for Boys* by Conn and Hal Iggulden and enjoy it with your sons. I guarantee there's great stuff in there you've never imagined trying.

Give them balance.

- Don't allow disrespect—of you, themselves, or others. Give them the opportunity to learn how to treat a lady, as they show you respect.
- Build their confidence as men. Provide them with healthy male role models. Point out positive characteristics in the men both you and your sons know. Place a high value on marriage and healthy male-female relationships. Involve them in male group activities like athletics and scouting.
- Hold the line as you teach them responsibility. Remember that you're raising a future leader. Don't excuse misbehavior or rude behavior. Be sure to set limits, and abide by them.
- As your sons grow, give them some space but always let them know you love them.

A single woman who is successful in raising multiple sons is *strong enough* to set boundaries, *perceptive enough* to sense when something is wrong, and *wise enough* to know when to stand back. The number of men raised without fathers in our culture is rising. We may not be able to change that, but we can positively affect the next generation of leaders. You can be part of that future as you raise today's boys to be representatives of character, strength, and honor.

Notes

Introduction

1. Stephen James and David Thomas, *Wild Things: The Art of Nurturing Boys* (Carol Stream, IL: Tyndale, 2009), 244.
2. William S. Pollack, *Real Boys: Rescuing Our Boys from the Myths of Boyhood* (New York: Random House, 1998), 81.

Chapter 1: Great Expectations

1. Dan Kindlon and Michael Thompson, *Raising Cain: Protecting the Emotional Life of Boys* (New York: Ballantine, 1999), 116.
2. James C. Dobson, *Bringing up Boys: Practical Advice and Encouragement for Those Shaping the Next Generation of Men* (Carol Stream, IL: Tyndale, 2005), 36.
3. Stephen James and David Thomas, *Wild Things: The Art of Nurturing Boys* (Carol Stream, IL: Tyndale, 2009), 245.
4. Susan Gilbert, *A Field Guide to Boys and Girls: Differences, Similarities, Cutting Edge Information Every Parent Needs to Know* (New York: HarperCollins, 2000), 14–19.
5. Ibid., 51–54.
6. James and Thomas, *Wild Things*, 115.

Chapter 2: The Magnet Syndrome (aka Sibling Rivalry)

1. Susan Gilbert, *A Field Guide to Boys and Girls: Differences, Similarities, Cutting Edge Information Every Parent Needs to Know* (New York: HarperCollins, 2000), 51–52

2. Frank J. Sulloway, *Born to Rebel: Birth Order, Family Dynamics, and Creative Lives* (New York: Vintage, 1997), 214.

3. T. Berry Brazelton, *Understanding Sibling Rivalry: The Brazelton Way* (Cambridge, MA: Da Capo Press, 2005), 64

4. Jane Mersky Leder, *Brothers and Sisters: How They Shape Our Lives* (New York: St. Martin's Press, 1991), 39.

5. Gilbert, *Field Guide to Boys and Girls*, 28–29.

6. Francine Klagsbrun, *Mixed Feelings: Love, Hate, Rivalry, and Reconciliation Among Brothers and Sisters* (New York: Bantam, 1992), 114.

7. Leder, *Brothers and Sisters*, 40.

Chapter 3: Intentional Parenting

1. Meg Meeker, *Boys Should Be Boys: Seven Secrets to Raising Healthy Sons* (Washington, DC: Regnery, 2008), 13.

2. James C. Dobson, *Bringing up Boys: Practical Advice and Encouragement for Those Shaping the Next Generation of Men* (Carol Stream, IL: Tyndale, 2005), 6–7.

3. Dan Kindlon and Michael Thompson, *Raising Cain: Protecting the Emotional Life of Boys* (New York: Ballantine, 1999), 130.

4. Dobson, *Bringing Up Boys*, 218–19.

5. James C. Dobson, *Parenting Isn't for Cowards: Dealing Confidently with the Frustrations of Child-Rearing* (Waco: Word Books, 1987), 104.

6. Meg Meeker, *Boys Should Be Boys*, 16.

7. Vicki Courtney, *Your Boy: Raising a Godly Son in an Ungodly World* (Nashville: B&H Publishing, 2006), 73–82.

8. Tim Shoemaker, *Dangerous Devotions for Guys: Dare to Live Your Faith* (Loveland, CO: Group Publishing, 2009).

Chapter 4: The Education of Boys

1. Kathy Hirsh-Pasek and Roberta Michnick Golinkoff, *Einstein Never Used Flash Cards: How Our Children Really Learn* (New York: Rodale, 2003), 214.
2. Conn Iggulden and Hal Iggulden, *The Dangerous Book for Boys* (New York: HarperCollins, 2007), xi.
3. Richard Louv, *Last Child in the Woods: Saving Our Children from Nature-Deficit Disorder* (Chapel Hill, NC: Algonquin Books, 2005), 34.
4. Michael Gurian, *The Wonder of Girls: Understanding the Hidden Nature of Our Daughters* (New York: Pocket Books, 2002), 57.
5. Statistics are found in "Boys at School," an interview with William Pollack (author of Real Boys), FamilyEducation, http://school.familyeducation.com/gender-studies/school-psychology/38493.html (accessed October 8, 2009) and "Understanding and Raising Boys: Boys in School" PBSParents, http://www.pbs.org/parents/raisingboys/school.html (accessed October 8, 2009).
6. Cheryl L. Erwin, *The Everything Parent's Guide to Raising Boys* (Avon: Adams Media, 2006), 184.
7. Meg Meeker, *Boys Should Be Boys: Seven Secrets to Raising Healthy Sons* (Washington, DC: Regnery, 2008), 185.

Chapter 5: Boy Talk

1. Cheryl L. Erwin, *The Everything Parent's Guide to Raising Boys* (Avon: Adams Media, 2006), 48–49.
2. Dan Kindlon and Michael Thompson, *Raising Cain: Protecting the Emotional Life of Boys* (New York: Ballantine, 1999), 16.
3. James C. Dobson, *Bringing up Boys: Practical Advice and Encouragement for Those Shaping the Next Generation of Men* (Carol Stream, IL: Tyndale, 2005), 96.
4. Ibid., 92.

5. Miriam Weinstein, *The Surprising Power of Family Meals: How Eating Together Makes Us Smarter, Stronger, Healthier and Happier* (New York: Bantam, 2006), 35.
6. Ibid.
7. Kindlon and Thompson, *Raising Cain*, 38–39.
8. Ibid., 17.
9. Adam J. Cox, *Boys of Few Words: Raising Our Sons to Communicate and Connect* (New York: Guilford Press, 2006), 11.
10. Ibid., 305.

Chapter 6: The Big O's—Order and Organization

1. Cheryl L. Erwin, *The Everything Parent's Guide to Raising Boys* (Avon: Adams Media, 2006), 223.
2. Ibid.
3. James C. Dobson, *Bringing up Boys: Practical Advice and Encouragement for Those Shaping the Next Generation of Men* (Carol Stream, IL: Tyndale, 2005), 230.
4. Leif G. Terdal and Patricia Kennedy, *Raising Sons Without Fathers: A Woman's Guide to Parenting Strong, Successful Boys* (Secaucus, NJ: Carol Publishing Group, 1996), 52.

Chapter 7: Media in a Young Man's Life

1. Meg Meeker, *Boys Should Be Boys: Seven Secrets to Raising Healthy Sons* (Washington, DC: Regnery, 2008), 57–58.
2. Ibid., 25.
3. Jonathan Rogers, "How Stories Do Their Work on Us," The Rabbit Room, October 23, 2008, http://www.rabbitroom.com/?p=1104#more-1104. Quoted by permission.
4. Ibid.
5. Adam J. Cox, *Boys of Few Words: Raising Our Sons to Communicate and Connect* (New York: Guilford Press, 2006), 234.
6. Sigmund Brouwer, "Hook the Reluctant Reader," Sigmund Brouwer Kids, September 23, 2007, http://www.sigmundbrouwerkids.com/archives/9. Quoted by permission.

7. Ibid.

8. David Dutwin, *Unplug Your Kids: A Parent's Guide to Raising Happy, Active, and Well-Adjusted Children in the Digital Age* (Cincinnati: Adams Media Corporation, 2009), 20–21.

9. Nancy W. Dickey, "TV and Babies: Should Viewers—Be This Young?" quoted in "A Guide to Managing Televisions: Tips for Your Family," written and compiled by Kyla Boyse, updated July 2009, University of Michigan Health System, http://www.med.umich.edu/yourchild/topics/managetv.htm.

Chapter 8: Growing Respect

1. Michael Gurian, *The Purpose of Boys: Helping Our Sons Find Meaning, Significance, and Direction in Their Lives* (Hoboken, NJ: John Wiley & Sons, Inc., 2009), 23, 40–42.

2. Robert Lewis, *Raising a Modern-Day Knight: A Father's Role in Guiding His Son to Authentic Manhood* (Carol Stream, IL: Tyndale, 2007), 66.

Chapter 9: A Band of Brothers

1. "Americans' Circle of Friends Is Shrinking" American Sociological Association press release, June 16, 2006, http://www.asanet.org/press/20060616.cfm.

Want more?

Visit www.OutnumberedMom.com to receive
- Links to helpful resources and Web sites.
- The Outnumbered Mom newsletter.
- More hope-filled stories from Laura and other moms.
- Information on how to contact Laura for speaking engagements.

"My purpose is that they may be encouraged in heart and united in love."
—Colossians 2:2